THE EMPOWERED SOUL

GUIDANCE & INSPIRATION TO CREATE A LIFE YOU LOVE

HARMESCH KAUR

Copyright © 2022 Harmesch Kaur

All rights reserved.

CW01375877

For My Soul

Dear Hannah

Thank you so much for
supporting me and my book!
Happy Reading!

love
Harmesch
/x.

TABLE OF CONTENTS

HOW TO USE THIS BOOK

THIS IS NOT a 'how-to' or 'should-do' book. Too often, we read books like this and set them aside, either because they might feel too prescriptive or overwhelming — or because they're not in total alignment with who we are or what we're looking for.

Instead, I wrote this book to serve as a guide to help you create a life you'll love. Only you hold the reins, the key 'intel' needed to create your own roadmap. This book gives you permission to forge your own way.

We'll journey together through this book in four key parts:

- **Part 1:** The Soul (Chapters 1-5)

- **Part 2:** The Practices (Chapters 6-8)

- **Part 3:** The Challenges (Chapters 9-10)

- **Part 4:** The Way Forward (Chapters 11-14)

With each part, you have at your disposal a collection of chapters — sprinkled with examples from my own story — to determine where you are now, identify changes to make, and learn how to make them.

Each chapter includes prompts, or Soul Activations, to encourage you to reflect on what you've read and create your go-forward plan. There are 100+ prompts in total. While the number of exercises varies per chapter, you'll find the bulk of the deep work comes in Chapters 6-9. So, I encourage you to take your time. Consider treating this book as a workbook, allotting one or two chapters per week. Allow yourself to dig deep and pace yourself. This is important work.

I have provided space to record your answers for each prompt, but you may want a journal to write down any additional thoughts. Journalling can help you see how far you've come and where you want to go.

Also, I don't want you to take your responses too seriously! Our Souls like to play and have fun. So I want you to have fun with your Soul. Take delight in dreaming and creating visions for yourself in all the different areas of your life. There are no right or wrong answers. This is about *you and your Soul* and the contract you've had with each other since birth.

You can find a list of resources at the end of this book that have helped me create the life I'm living today — and you might find they help you too.

A note here on the terms 'Universe' and 'Soul' that I use throughout this book: I don't follow a particular religion (I have been raised in the Sikh religion), and so don't pray to or revere any religious leaders or gods. My faith lies in the Universe. Wherever you see the word Universe, feel free to replace it with who or what you believe in: God, Source, Guru, Buddha — you get the idea.

For me, the word Soul represents me in this lifetime. It is that part of me that cannot be seen or touched but is my eternal self reincarnated at this particular time and place. I think of my Soul as energy guided by the Universe, driving my human self to experience everything it came here for. However you name your deepest, most authentic self, you can interchange it with the term 'Soul' throughout this book.

So, are you ready to DREAM BIG, create a life you love, and have fun in the process? Read on, and let's get started!

INTRODUCTION

And [let it] direct your passion with reason, that your passion may live through its own daily resurrection, and like the phoenix rises above its own ashes.

— Khalil Gibran

HAVE YOU ever envisioned a new life for yourself — a life that would fulfil your dreams but feels so far removed from your reality that it doesn't seem possible? Have you ever thought, 'This way of life isn't working for me anymore!' but don't know how to take the first step to change?

Or, perhaps you've been feeling a bit lacklustre lately or lacking purpose, knowing there's something more for you than what you've experienced so far in your life.

Here's a secret: We all get to create our lives, but not all of us choose to accept this challenge. If you're yearning for true transformation, to tap into the great something more that life can offer, to accept the challenge to re-architect your life, then this book will help you listen to your Soul to get there.

You might be familiar with the phoenix, the immortal bird associated with Greek mythology that's said to burn to ash and is reborn brighter and better than before. I believe our lives can be reborn just like the phoenix. They can be burned to ash and rebuilt.

Everything happens for a reason.

It's out of my control.

What will be, will be.

There must be more to life than this.

I'm guessing you've probably heard or said these phrases more times than you care to admit. When you continually 'let life happen' or don't take action when things don't go how you'd like, you're not taking part in creating your own life. And when you're not taking an active role in your life, it's easy to become frustrated, resentful, and depressed.

Perhaps you're living a life that you let family, friends, and society dictate. Maybe you're happy to go along with it because you don't want to stand out or cause trouble. It's understandable to want to fit in, to not upset the world order. And this world order makes it easy to conform, doesn't it? We're conditioned to 'perform' life in a certain way, and our choices might be frowned upon or ridiculed when we don't follow that path.

Have you ever been asked the following questions that challenged how you live your life?

Why don't you want to get married?

You don't want to work a corporate job?

Why would you want to go there on your holiday?

Why wouldn't you want to have children?

How did you respond? Many of us might revert to the 'norm' and step back into line with society and those around us — and in the process, we lose ourselves.

But some of us may decide to listen to what our Soul desires. It took me many years to finally tune into my Soul and gain the confidence to live the life I'm meant to. Let me share part of my story with you.

MY PHOENIX EXPERIENCE

I haven't wholly followed the traditional path that my family, friends, culture, and society wanted for me, but it took a long time to finally blaze my own trail. I've had my share of moments when I went along with situations that didn't feel right. I've worked for too many years in jobs I didn't enjoy. I've stayed in friendships and relationships that were draining my energy and affecting my mental and physical health. And I've people-pleased like a trooper because I had no idea how to love myself and instead sought validation and approval from those around me.

This kind of behaviour could only continue for a finite time because a voice inside me was getting increasingly angry. I was becoming frustrated and burnt out because I wasn't living the life that would bring *me* the most enjoyment and fulfilment. Instead, I was merely existing.

I'd wake up each morning and go to my 9-to-5 job, join in office banter, talk about TV shows and what was for dinner, and gossip about other people. As soon as I clocked off, I'd be back on a train home to an evening of watching TV, numbing my emotions with food, and ignoring how depressed and sad I felt. Of course, social events, family gatherings, work commitments, and holidays served as a distraction. But on the whole, this is how my life had panned out.

From a very early age, I was taught that there was an expected path to my life: Go to school, maybe attend university, get a job, find a partner, get married, have children, and that's it. I would have the perfect life.

Despite my early efforts to follow this narrow view of life, there came a time when I believed there *was* something more for me. I *wanted* something more. I just didn't know what it was or how to get it. I felt stuck.

As a result, I spent over twenty years struggling with depression and anxiety. I always felt like I was living to triage immediate issues rather than enjoy my life. I repeatedly made the same mistakes — in friendships, jobs, and life decisions. It became a huge energy drain, and I didn't seem to have the joy for life I'd seen others experience.

I remember being called moody, dull, and unhappy, and these remarks made me feel worse than I already did. Unfortunately, when I went to my doctor, knowing something wasn't right, mental health problems weren't openly spoken about in the way they are today.

I was offered counselling, consisting of six weekly sessions for fifty minutes each. They barely made a scratch in the issues and emotions I was facing. I had to raise a complaint with my doctor before I was taken seriously about my depression. And then, I spent eighteen months with a psychiatrist and community psychiatric nurse, trying to help me out of the pit of despair I was in.

The medication they prescribed helped minimise negative emotions. I no longer felt hopeless, sad, desperate, angry, or frustrated, but I also didn't feel the positive feelings I expected. Where was the happiness, hope, joy, and delight?

Even though I had sought medical help, my depression wasn't improving. My uncle suggested a working holiday in New Zealand, where he and his wife lived. I accepted his offer to visit but didn't want to travel to the other side of the world reliant on anti-depressants.

My doctor advised against stopping my medication, but the community psychiatric nurse helped me slowly reduce my dosage until I could stop taking it. People noticed the positive difference in me almost immediately. Maybe my change in mood was partly due to the thought of escaping everything and flying off to the other side of the world. Whatever it was, I felt lighter.

Being in New Zealand made me feel free. It was easy to hide my mental health issues because no one knew who I was, and no one suspected I'd been in the darkest period of my life a few months earlier. I made a choice not to allow my mental health issues to spoil the experience I was having. It wasn't always easy because, as the saying goes, 'Wherever you go, there you are.' My depression didn't fully disappear in New Zealand, but while I was there, I felt happier than I had in a long time. And it was because I *chose* to be happy and to let myself experience what was coming my way.

I became spontaneous, travelling to places I'd never been. I spoke to people I didn't know, whereas before, I would have been too scared to approach people for fear of rejection. I played along with the Universe.

I came back from my travels a slightly different person: more outspoken, more willing to experience new things, and more *willing* to be happy. I felt fixed. I was a different version of myself, and the box I had put my mental health issues inside stayed closed for a while.

Roll on a few years, and my friend Depression decided to come and stay again, this time bringing its 'plus one,' Anxiety. I'd spent years building a life after my mental illness, so the depression really floored me this time. I was constantly crying, abusing alcohol, engaging in unhealthy relationships, and trying to destroy myself and the cloud hanging over my head. To make matters worse, I was in a toxic work environment that helped me hide my behaviours because my co-workers seemed equally unhappy.

When the suicidal thoughts came, I knew I had to do something. Like the proverbial phoenix, my life had completely crashed and burned. I couldn't carry on like this, and I definitely didn't want to go further into the black abyss again. This time, I chose to go to private therapy. I knew that if I wanted this to work, I had to have consequences; at the time, money was that consequence. Paying for private therapy kept me accountable. I was lucky to find someone who truly saw and heard me. Nearly a year later, I had worked through many of the issues that had made me unhappy.

In 2019, I'd met up for lunch with ex-colleagues at one of London's underground bars. I shared that I was on a self-imposed six-week break from drinking so I wouldn't get questioned or judged about sticking to my soft drink. If I hadn't told this little white lie, that afternoon would have ended like many other lunchtimes or after-work drinks: I'd get drunk because of pressure to keep up with the pace of drinking, manage to get myself home, and then spend the rest of the evening curled up on my sofa or in my bed.

British drinking and pub culture are real, so alcohol has been a major player in my life. It's also a big part of my Punjabi culture, and I grew up watching men getting paralytically drunk at weddings and social gatherings. Being female didn't stop me from following what the men were doing, and I soon found opportunities to drink with friends outside of my culture.

I never hid my drinking from my parents. They didn't like it, but I wanted to be honest in case a relative or family friend saw me out with a drink in my hand. Alcohol helped me relax so I could socialise, numbing me from the challenges I faced. I wasn't an alcoholic by any means, but I had a very toxic relationship with drinking. I thought I was doing okay because I wasn't as 'out of control' as others and managed to easily recover from a hangover.

Just a few months before, at the end of 2018, a job change brought a surprising life-changing experience. I was fortunate to be offered a role with a company working with the Australian Stock Exchange. I wouldn't have to move to Australia, but instead, I was able to work remotely from my home in London. The only difference was that my 9-to-5 was turned on its head; I worked from four in the afternoon until two the next morning.

I no longer had time to meet friends and old colleagues for after-work drinks. This job gave me so much time, and my days were my own. It would have to be during the day if I wanted to meet anyone. It meant that I was no longer going out drinking several times a week.

My relationship with alcohol improved. I couldn't drink during the week because I was working, which provided time and space for my mind to get clear. I realised I'd been living most of my days in a foggy haze because of the drinking. But anyone who has gone sober or had a significant break from alcohol will tell you how much clearer their mind felt. This was a new feeling for me.

For over ten years, I'd not only been destroying my health, but I had been putting my life on hold. I'd gone from job to job to increase my salary and meet new colleagues to socialise and drink with. I didn't have a partner or children, and I spent my weeknights drinking and my weekends recovering.

This new job and the way I was working gave me the freedom to think about what I wanted and where I wanted to be in my life. So, that afternoon in the bar, I was finally confident enough to declare that I wouldn't be working in the City *or* the corporate world by the time I was fifty.

That was only three-and-a-half years away! How was I going to manage to give up my well-paid job? I didn't particularly enjoy my work; it was sometimes stressful, but the social aspect and salary kept me motivated. It was great declaring what I *wasn't* going to be doing, but I didn't know what I *did* want to do. I had no clue what type of job I could do that wouldn't require me to start at the bottom again and give up my current comfortable lifestyle.

But then something remarkable happened. Once I made that declaration, opportunities came along to prepare me for a new path. I eventually didn't have to work in the City anymore, and I could live the way I wanted and leave the rat race behind. The Universe was listening intently that afternoon. It put ideas into my head and helped me gain confidence to execute those ideas.

My work contract in Australia was only for a one-year term, and I had an idea about how I wanted to end my corporate career. In late 2019, before my contract ended, I declared I only wanted to work four days a week. The remaining day of the work week, I wanted to focus on the life I yearned to create for myself. It was another declaration to the Universe about what I wanted, and the Universe was happy to play along. In 2020, I returned to a previous employer on a four-day a week freelance contract, getting paid more than I did for a prior five-day a week contract.

Then the pandemic hit the global stage. I was fortunate to keep my job, though I was moved to a different team. The pandemic was an annoyance for some, but it was a godsend for me. It gave me time and space to work on myself, and I connected with people across the globe —

people I may never have met if I wasn't forced to work from home and spend time in solitude. It presented opportunities that may never have come my way. Most importantly, it gave me the gift of looking at my life and deciding how I wanted to live it.

I finally felt ready to rise from my ashes again.

IT'S TIME TO EMPOWER YOUR SOUL

Even after therapy, I continued my inner exploration, including working with life coaches (spoiler alert: I also trained as one!). In talking with friends I made in my coaching programmes and yoga teacher training, I realised that while therapy helped me work through my trauma, it didn't help me rebuild my life.

Therapy can help us discover why we feel the way we do and pinpoint what keeps us locked in a prison of destructive behaviour. It doesn't necessarily give us an action plan or help to set goals to change our jobs, or financial situation, or get in touch with our spiritual selves.

You are there to talk, not to create. *I want you to create.*

In this book, I'll teach you to take the things you've learned about yourself on your life journey so far and use them to create a life you love: a life you never want to walk away from and a life that keeps evolving just as you do.

I'll arm you with the same tools I've used to create my life as it is now. I want you to feel that you are living, not just existing, and I want you to feel supported.

And don't fear: I'm not going to ask you to leave your job or your relationship (unless that's what you want!). Instead, I've set up this book to help you make incremental changes for living a life that brings you joy every day.

Mental illness was my wake-up call to finally create the life I deserved. For you, the catalyst might be watching a relationship break down, losing someone close, or leaving a job or business.

If a major life event has taken you down, I want you to rise again like a phoenix and become the next version — a *better version* — of yourself. Your journey to that version doesn't have to mean dramatic life changes. Small changes can impact your life more than one significant change would. I know because many small changes I've made have affected my life and relationships in subtle but transformative ways.

All of us can change our lives once we decide to do so, but it doesn't happen overnight. It's something we have to work on every day. We may move forward and slip back a little. And that's okay. Life is all about ebbs and flows.

The key is to keep tuning into your Soul for direction. The more you learn to listen, the more you empower your Soul to create a life you love. I hope this book provides you with the guidance and inspiration to do just that.

PART ONE

The Soul

CHAPTER ONE:
BARRIERS OR GATEWAYS?

Your task is not to seek for love, but merely to seek and find all the barriers within yourself that you have built against it.

— Rumi

MANY OF US spend our lives on auto-pilot and don't consciously create or participate in the life we want. And that's because many of us aren't taught how. We may follow guidance from our parents, grandparents, teachers, employers, family, and friends. In doing so, we slip into patterns of thinking and being that have us living precisely the same way as everyone else in society.

Got a good job? Check!

Got a girlfriend / boyfriend / wife / husband? Check!

Got a home for you and the family? Check!

Go on holiday each year? Check!

If you have some or all of these things, that's not necessarily bad. Some people are content with this prescribed way of life.

But I know *you're* not content. That's why you sought out this book.

I suspect you want to discover how to bring more joy into your life. Maybe you had it at some point, but that joy and excitement you used to feel seems to have gone on a holiday of its own.

Perhaps you want to know how to wake up with the same energy and glow you've seen in others. They seem to glide through life and new adventures while you're stuck in the mundane with another pile of washing to sort through.

In this book, we'll address new concepts and walk through exercises to empower your Soul to live the life it wants and deserves and is here for. This said, be prepared to encounter barriers on your self-improvement journey. And you'll need to discern if something is really a barrier — or a gateway in disguise.

In the following sections of this chapter, we'll address how to reframe four 'barriers' that, on closer inspection, may actually be gateways to your success:

1. Crossing the Line of Decision

2. Reframing self-help culture

3. Not playing the guilt game

4. Exploring the benefits of counselling and coaching.

CROSSING THE LINE OF DECISION

When creating a life for yourself, you will encounter a Line of Decision between the old and the new. Your challenge is to step over that line. You get to walk up to the line, maybe start to slide your toes over the edge, but then you may return to where you currently are. You might step one foot over the line, only to hesitate and bring it back. And this can carry on at regular intervals in your life. Maybe you're afraid, full of doubts, or feel held back by others. Something is always there to prevent you (and all of us!) from crossing over that Line of Decision.

What does it take to cross the line? Some might say time, but it is actually having the courage to decide that the 'old' side of the line is no longer serving you. At this point, you'll want to see what the other side of the line has to offer.

Do you need to be ready? Not really. No amount of mindset change or safety nets will help you step over the line if you don't dare to do so.

It doesn't matter what this Line of Decision leads to: a job, a relationship, a home. One side will always represent your current reality, and the other side will reflect what you desire. And what you desire is usually better than what you have now — because who wishes for anything worse than what they currently have? Still, something can stop us from stepping over that line.

Sometimes a drastic event — losing a job, the death of a loved one, or health issues — may need to happen before we make the step across. Things we see as challenging are actually helping us to edge closer to that line. We're being pushed to make the step so that we can discover something better.

What happens if we never step over that line? Our current reality will never change. We'll continue to experience life as we are now and face the same challenges and frustrations that led us to walk up to the line in the first place. We may become a little more accepting of the situation, or we might numb ourselves to it. How long will we continue dragging ourselves through life because we think we have no choice but to stay where we are? The truth is there is always a choice, and only each one of us can make it for ourselves.

Crossing this Line of Decision can feel more daunting because often, we can't see what is on the other side. I believe that until you find the courage to step over, it won't be revealed to you. And that's the risk we all take. Is your life worth the risk? Do you want to experience something different? If you're feeling stuck in how your life is going, why, then, would you want to stay there?

I'll say one more thing about the line: it will never go away; it will always be there. We may have stepped over it once, but it will appear again one day, ready for us to step over again. That's how we grow and keep creating our life. Life will always manifest as a series of lines for us to decide whether to cross over or not.

Here's an example: I worked on technology projects for over a decade. I'd worked my way up the career ladder but never felt I was doing anything of actual worth to anyone. Even though these jobs were well-paid and gave me a lifestyle I enjoyed, I was still dissatisfied.

Like so many people in this world, I didn't particularly like my job, but I also didn't know what I wanted to do. So I stayed where I was or found a similar role in a different organisation, hoping I'd feel differently about what I was doing. I eventually realised that if I didn't start to explore my options, I'd be working in this type of role until I was replaced by younger employees or could no longer work. Not a life-affirming prospect!

I had to step over the line and discover what else the world had to offer me. It hasn't always been easy, but I'm further on my path. I know there will be more Lines of Decision to cross because that's how life works. What matters was that I decided to step over the line in the first place. And that's what matters most for you.

Take some time to work through the following prompts. Remember, there are no right or wrong answers.

1. What is the Line of Decision that you are contemplating crossing (there can be more than one)?

2. What do you feel stops you from stepping
    across this line or lines? Write an answer
    for each of these Lines of Decision.

3. How would it feel for you to cross that
    Line of Decision?

SELF-HELP IS NOT A DIRTY WORD

For some people, the phrase 'self-help' is a dirty word, somehow suggesting there's something wrong with them. So instead of getting help, they stick to the very life they're trying to change or improve.

But self-help *isn't* a dirty word. According to research firm Market Data Forecast, the self-help and personal development industry was worth USD 38.28 billion in 2019, expected to grow by a further 5.1% up until 2027. That's a lot of us with something 'wrong' using self-help and personal development tools! In fact, exploring self-help books was my entry point into learning how to look out for myself and not rely on others to change my life.

During my earlier depressive episodes, self-help books benefited me the most since I wasn't clear where else to turn. As I've already mentioned, in the late 1990s, mental health wasn't a subject widely spoken about in England, and resources were not readily available. Conversations, support, and resources have improved, and we're much more open about mental health — even though there is still a long way to go.

When I didn't know how a loved one, friend, or colleague would react to what I was going through, self-help books became a source of guidance, inspiration, and solace. I believe books, especially those covering self-help, come into our lives when we need them or are open to receiving what they have for us. The key is to remain open.

This book, which you might consider self-help, is simply a collection of my experiences in different areas of my life and how I have navigated them. I share the tools I've used and what has brought me results to give you ready access to create a new version of a life you'll love.

While you might not have experienced everything that I have, there may be certain situations that you resonate with. And you may try the tools in this book but not have the same results as me. I'll repeat: remain open. Let go of any preconceptions. The tools in this book aren't complicated — because people don't want to complicate their lives any more than they already are. And I know you don't want to, either! We all want simple, easy-to-use solutions that don't take up too much of our precious time.

Even though I put in the work to make it through the more challenging times, I haven't stopped reading self-help books. I still come across books that help me with whatever I am going through in my life. So, never be scared to turn to a self-help book because it may be the very thing that saves you in a time of need.

I've listed a few of my favourite books in the Resources chapter.

1. What are some of your favourite self-help books that have had a big impact on your life?

2. If you've never read a self-help book, what made you decide that this was the time to start exploring self-help in this way?

DON'T PLAY THE GUILT GAME

It seems to happen every time. As soon as we admit we're not completely satisfied with life, we begin to feel guilty because we can easily imagine people much worse off: the unhoused, those suffering from food poverty or long-term illness, and so on.

I recall jobs I resigned from but felt guilty about because I knew my colleagues would have to deal with the same stress I was leaving behind. I remember wanting to end friendships that weren't good for me but stayed because I didn't want to hurt the other person's feelings.

Does this sound familiar? When we realise that something in our life isn't right and needs to change — or that there must be something more for us — we can start to feel that guilt creep in. Who are we to change the *status quo* or disrupt others' lives because we want to be happy?

Thoughts like these can keep us stuck in our lives. Before we know it, another six weeks, five months, or ten years have passed. And we're still in the same situation wishing for the same things, but circumstances (or, more truthfully, *our choices*) have kept us where we are.

I don't want that for you. I want you to feel courageous enough to step outside your comfort zone and experience something that lights up your Soul and lets you pour into others from a full cup.

1. What guilt triggers pop up when you explore making a life change?

2. How can you reframe these triggers to recognise your personal growth is a priority over guilt?

EXPLORING COUNSELLING AND COACHING

Beyond books, counselling through a public health network or private sector is an incredible self-help tool. I've utilised both types of counselling, though private therapy brought the most significant change for me.

As I wrote in the Introduction, I was investing in myself, paying my own money each week to see a private therapist and talk. And talk. *And talk.* I spent nearly a year doing this with the most fantastic therapist. She helped me to see myself and not my illness. She also helped me deal with the challenges I had at the time, but I didn't feel that the counselling followed up with how to integrate what I learned into my life.

I've spoken to others who have felt the same. Therapy deals with what you are going through at that moment in time. It delves into your past to see why you might have gotten there. Once that answer is known, it's time to get on with your life. The therapist's job is done.

If you're a mental health professional reading this, please know I'm not saying counselling or therapy comes up short. I think therapy is changing along with the conversations on mental health. It can be life-saving, and it certainly was for me.

Counselling identified the root of some of my problems, but it didn't help me learn how to recalibrate my life with this new knowledge. It wasn't until I worked with a life coach that I realised what had been missing.

Coaching is a growing industry; you can hire a coach for almost anything, including money, sexual intimacy issues, parenting, business, or self-transformation. I hired my first coach because I wanted to work in the coaching industry — and everything I read told me I should get coached to be a coach. So I did. My coach was more like a friend I would meet up with for tea and a chat, but they also would call me out when I didn't do what I said I would.

Along with my interest in becoming a coach, I was trying to start a yoga business but felt overwhelmed with where to start. My coach helped me set goals, something I'd never done before, and then make action plans to achieve those goals. But the more I was coached, the more I realised I didn't want to be a yoga teacher. I remembered that coaching was the direction I wanted to take in the first place. Getting coached helped me to see where I was blocking myself and where I lacked confidence in what I was already doing.

That wasn't the last time I hired a coach. Since then, I'm rarely without some type of coach, whether it's to work on myself, my business, or to improve my coaching skills. And group programmes are a great way to get coached and learn from other participants because everyone brings something different to the group. They also tend to be a bit easier on the bank account!

I've tried several programmes, but one — a four-month programme called Stretch 22, with transformational leader Preston Smiles — helped me change my life. He'd been a mentor in a four-month business coaching programme I'd completed, and with other powerhouse coaches in his programme, I had a team of people ready to help me level up to who I was placed on earth to be.

That said, coaching is a serious endeavour, one that comes with a huge payoff if you're willing to invest in the work. You'll feel every emotion possible once you start to be coached, and I was not exempt. I cried, I was angry, and I was embarrassed. But most of all, I felt immense joy and peace. My confidence and self-belief grew so much that I knew I could no longer get distracted by what other people wanted from me.

That programme helped me learn to integrate my healing and prior therapy into my life. It provided the roadmap to put principles into practice. It didn't just show me where my issues were; it helped me move through them and emerge as a better version of myself. It gave me the tools to create my own solutions instead of sending me out into the world with my problems still attached to me.

That programme gave me back my power and helped me write this book.

Getting coached helps you draw out the answers you already have in yourself about what you want. It's not for everyone, but it can help you shift your life quicker than therapy. Breakthroughs can happen so quickly that you don't even see them coming! I can't count the times I've had that *a-ha* moment when I've realised I've changed because of what a coaching session revealed to me.

A good coach will call out your bullshit and nudge you to the way you need to go. They will show you the possibilities you may be blind to and help you believe in yourself and go after what you deserve in this life. If that's something you think will help you create the life you want, I encourage you to get a coach. I've listed some options in the Resources section.

I delight in seeing people transform as a result of coaching. I love how a mindset shift in one area can spill into other areas of a person's life. I get a rush seeing the pure joy on a person's face when they finally believe in themselves and their gifts. I appreciate the opportunity to watch people become the best version of themselves.

When a person is stuck in a life they think they have to lead forever, only to realise they can choose what they want to do, the result is almost spiritual. Watching someone step into their power, live by their own rules, and not worry about other people's opinions is a wonder to behold. Seeing people heal from years of trauma and become aware of the part they play in their own life can be one of the most joyful things to witness.

I'm not saying you have to get a coach, but from my own experience and witnessing the experiences of others, you would be showing yourself some real self-love by doing so.

1. Have you ever pursued counselling or coaching?

2. If you have, how did they benefit you?

3. If you've tried both, how did they differ for you?

4. If you haven't, what has stopped you from pursuing this type of self-development support?

FINAL THOUGHT

To create a life you love, it's important to discern if you've been viewing invitations and resources to move you toward building a life you love as barriers or gateways.

Once you embrace the ideas of crossing the Line of Decision, reframe self-help culture, stop playing the guilt game, and explore the benefits of counselling and coaching, you're ready to discover your Treasure Chest and start dreaming up all your life can be.

CHAPTER TWO:

DISCOVER YOUR TREASURE CHEST

All you can possibly need or desire is already yours.

— Neville Goddard

I WANT TO INTRODUCE you to the Treasure Chest. I first heard this term in a one-to-one session with a life coach who is a manifestation queen. Once she explained the concept, it made perfect sense — and it has helped me intentionally focus my desires to create the life I want. It can do the same for you, and I'll explain how in this chapter.

The Treasure Chest is exactly what it sounds like: a chest of treasure, *your* treasure. It contains everything your Soul desires and knows is available to you. The Universe has already given you everything you want in your life: a dream house, car, holiday, job, relationship, family, and more. All you have to do is access your Treasure Chest.

Of course, this Treasure Chest isn't something we can physically touch or see, but it's there, waiting for you to take action and claim the things you say you want.

'So what is stopping me?', you might ask. It comes down to your belief that you can access the gifts in your Treasure Chest and live the life you desire.

This realisation isn't just true for you. It's true for all of us, but not all of us might *believe* we are worthy of the things our Treasure Chest contains.

Our Treasure Chests also include our emotional needs: support from loved ones, the feeling of belonging or being loved, or the comfort of being in a community. Yet, it's so easy to get stuck in mindsets, behaviours, and situations that keep us from meeting those needs.

We also might believe we must struggle and work hard for what we want. We may assume that only those who put in the effort, work long hours, save money, and do all the 'right' things, will be rewarded with the life they dream of. Or, perhaps we buy into the lie that everything worth having is not easy. This way of thinking blocks these blessings coming to us — blessings that are, by the way, already ours.

I used to limit myself to these false beliefs, particularly in my career. I believed that to get anything in my life, I had to knuckle down, work harder than everyone else, to progress to the next stage in my job — and *only then* would I get the recognition and salary for which I was working so hard. That, in turn, would mean that I could afford the house and car that society told me I *had* to have.

Yet after years of hard work, I received little to no salary increase, but the expectation to work harder and longer hours remained. The long working hours started to take their toll, but I still dragged myself out of bed each morning. I desperately wanted to leave my job and knew there must be a better way to make money and live life.

The Universe hears everything. It listened to what I wanted and was kind enough to put opportunities in my path. I met people with no 'job security' but were getting paid much more as freelancers for doing the same full-time work I was doing. At the time — being risk-averse and listening to others rather than my Soul (and the Universe) — I stayed in the job that kept me in the very situation I wanted to escape.

And it wasn't just the one time. The Universe kept sending me these opportunities, but I wasn't acting on the signs. Even though I never took these opportunities, the Universe was not deterred by my lack of belief.

Through my thoughts, I had told the Universe what I wanted — and so it kept sending me opportunities and challenges in the hope I would finally take what was presented.

My job was full of conflict, boredom, and expectations that didn't align with who I was. But did I take notice? Like hell I did! I was still in the mindset that I had to struggle through tough times to get to the good stuff. This internal conflict continued for most of my career until I reached a place where my work environment was so toxic that I had to find a way out for my health.

I finally took the risk of leaving a well-paid permanent role where I wasn't learning anything or moving up the career ladder and accepted a six-month contract role where I would be thrown into the deep end. It meant I would be learning not only job skills but also personal skills. That action gave me the confidence to continue walking away from jobs that didn't feel right or weren't serving my growth. Over the past fifteen years, my work history may have looked like I couldn't commit to a job, but every single role I took (including returning to a permanent position for a short while) was a lesson in my growth, leading me closer to *my* Treasure Chest.

UNLOCKING YOUR TREASURE CHEST

Perhaps you're reading this and thinking, 'Where's *my* Treasure Chest? Where are the things I want in my life? I'm always asking for them, so why haven't they shown up yet?'

My question is: What have you done to get what you're after? Is it something you've spoken into the Universe or kept hidden in your heart? The Universe can't hear you if you remain silent.

The Universe is constantly directing you by putting opportunities and choices before you. Still, you won't be on the path to your Treasure Chest if you're not noticing those opportunities or asking for things that lead you away from what you *really* want. You will, in fact, be steering yourself further away from it.

Let's say you're single and desire to find a partner. You can ask for all sorts of things, but if you don't get down to the specifics, the Universe will put all types of partners in your space. You then get to choose, increasing the chance that the partner you select is not the best match. Before long, they start to exhibit certain traits or behaviours that don't align with your beliefs or expectations. You leave the relationship and look for something new.

You now know these certain traits or behaviours are not welcome in a new relationship. So, the Universe listens and narrows down your selection, and you pick another partner. Luckily, those undesirable traits and behaviours aren't present, but other equally undesirable traits and behaviours appear. So, you leave that relationship and go on to the next one and the next one. Eventually, you'll find a partner who meets your desires, or you'll choose to compromise.

This type of trial and error is great if we're aware and speaking to our Soul, but those not doing that end up staying in relationships that aren't in alignment for various reasons: loneliness, not feeling good enough for anyone else, trauma, and more. I'm trying to illustrate that the Universe will eventually lead you to your Treasure Chest — as long as you listen to your Soul instead of making decisions from a logical place.

There is no right or wrong decision or choice. Instead, we make choices in or out of alignment with our greatest good. That's why we sometimes get feelings of unease when we've made a particular choice. Or, we find ourselves harbouring regret or resentment because if we were doing something aligned with our greatest good, we'd feel more positive about it and what it was bringing into our life.

I used to believe that I was in control of my destiny, that I was the one in control of my life and what could happen in it. But over time, I've realised my old belief isn't true. My decisions didn't align with my greatest good, and my choices impacted many areas of my life.

So, the Universe would redirect me, presenting me with challenges until I got to a place to make the 'right' decision. I started noticing changes when I did this and felt more joy and peace. Reflecting on how I'd gotten to that point, I realised the Universe was guiding me, and I was listening to what my Soul wanted at that moment. By experiencing how these situations, opportunities, and challenges have played out, I've become able to trust the Universe to keep showing me the way to my Treasure Chest. I continue to connect with my Soul and listen to what it wants and knows is true for me.

I want you to listen deeply to your Soul for this exercise. Try to tap into what your Soul wants you to know.

1. What does your Treasure Chest hold? What would you like it to hold?

2. What beliefs have been holding you back from receiving the things in your Treasure Chest?

3. Is there anything in your life that your Treasure Chest has already given you?

A DREAM WITHOUT ACTION IS JUST A WISH

We all want to live our dream lives, which can look different for each of us. We all *deserve* to live our dream life. Yet, many of us are too afraid or don't know where to start creating it. So, we carry on as passengers in our somewhat mediocre lives. We keep going to the job we don't enjoy. We entertain the friends and family who drain us. We put up with the demands of others. We stay in relationships that no longer fulfil us.

Yet, every so often, we allow ourselves to dream again. We open up that little box in our head that holds our dream job, dream house, dream relationship, dream business, dream family, and dream environment. We allow ourselves to pretend that we are the main character in that life, gliding along with joy and happiness, with not a care in the world. We continue this fantasy until someone or something interrupts our reverie, and we're quickly brought back to earth to contend with life's routine.

I don't share this to depress you but to show you a piece of reality. Why? Because you're not the only one who sometimes wants out of your current life or desires to create a new one. Millions of people feel the same way, but not all will have the courage to take the first step in finding their Treasure Chest.

For many years, I felt there was something more for me in this world — but there was always something holding me back from finding and holding on to it. I've had glimpses of it, but it always seemed to slip my grasp, leaving me frustrated and wondering whether I should be content with what I had.

I spent too many years in jobs that provided no progression or fulfilment, nor did I consider them helpful to society. I've spent too many years keeping quiet so that I would please others. I've spent too many years striving to live the way that most of society does, only to find it's not how I want my life to be. I've spent too many years allowing toxic relationships to take up my time and energy. And I've spent many years trying to save everyone around me rather than ensuring I saved myself first.

Can you relate? If so, I am here to tell you that we can't create and live our dream lives when we're putting all our efforts into helping those around us create and live *their* dream life. Read that again.

If you're like me, there comes the point where you will no longer want just to dream — because dreaming without taking action is just wishing. You won't want to spend another moment wishing that your dream life will be handed to you in a gold box containing everything you've hoped for. You'll want to live that life now. You'll no longer want to be the passenger. You'll want to be the one driving yourself forward into that dream life. You'll want to experience all the joy and happiness life has available. You'll want to build a life that nurtures you and those around you. You'll want that dream career or business. You'll want a relationship that supports you and grows with you.

And you can have it — as long as you take action. No one else will do it for you because they're also trying to get to the same place you are: *their* dream life.

I don't want you to take as long as I did to get to that place. Full transparency: the dream life doesn't happen overnight. I'm still on my journey to get there, but I'm having fun and enjoying every moment! I'm a lot further along than I was when all I could think was, 'There has to be something more to life than this!'

I want you to dream, to play, and to have fun. I want you to create the life you've dreamed of. And if that dream changes along the way, that's great because there is nothing to say that you have to stick to that one dream. It's your life, after all!

Happy dreaming and happy creating. Remember, without action, a dream is just a wish.

1. I want you to have a little fun here. If you could wave a magic wand and have the life of your dreams, what would that look like? Get specific and include details! Where would you love to live? What would your ideal day look like? Would you be working or creating income differently?

2. What simple actions could you take to start making those dreams a reality?

DREAM AND DECIDE — BIG!

Now that I've challenged you to start dreaming, I want to know: How big do you let yourself dream? I ask because many of us tend to keep our dreams very small. They may seem significant to us, but actually, they aren't. That's because we don't believe we'll achieve those dreams. So, we only allow ourselves to imagine what we *think* we can realise in our lives.

Ask yourself this: does limiting your dreams benefit you? Of course not! By keeping your goals small, you keep yourself and your world small. Soon, you'll likely start wondering if there's something more out there for you, just as I did. Dreaming big allows you to see possibilities and envision what your life could be like if you wanted it to be.

There was a time in my life when I didn't have much hope for my outcome. I've mentioned already that I was diagnosed as clinically depressed. I didn't feel joy or happiness. And I didn't know whether I'd ever feel those positive vibes people kept talking about. At that time, my only dream was to get better, whatever getting better meant. I only knew that I wanted to experience more joy and have hope for my future.

It was a very vague yet narrow dream. I always thought I'd live in the same place I grew up and I'd only ever see the same people. I never let my mind expand beyond what I already knew. I kept my hopes small because I didn't think I'd be able to get anything more than what I already had and a little bit extra.

But when I did 'get better,' my dreams became bigger. I wanted to get a specific job; I didn't want to stay in an administrative position for the rest of my life. I wanted to earn a certain amount of money because I wanted to be able to afford nice things, go to nice places, and have memorable experiences. I put in the work to do that, and I got what I wanted — sort of.

Why do I say sort of? Because my dreams were small. Soon enough, I felt there must be more than I had. I allowed myself to dream about living in a beautiful part of London and owning property. And it happened. I worked hard and got what I wanted. But again, it wasn't enough. I knew there had to be something more.

By keeping my dreams small, I constantly wanted to find something else once I'd achieved that dream. Yes, there was celebration and satisfaction in these things that I did, and for a while, they excited me. But once I had them, where was there left to go?

I started to learn that dreaming big keeps me scared and excited and gives me drive in my life. It gives me hope and satisfaction as I look to these big dreams because the journey to get to them is more important than the dream itself.

In dreaming small, we only expand ourselves a certain amount. When we dream big, we receive greater challenges and situations, which keep us on the path of growth to create our lives.

These big dreams and the extraordinary life we are after can sometimes scare us. And sometimes, we might retreat from what the Universe is giving us. We may want to slow down because our big dreams are hurtling towards us at a pace we can't control. Or, maybe we want to decide how and when these dreams show up for us. But that isn't how the Universe works.

The Universe will co-create these with you as soon as you set your intention for your big dreams. I believe the Universe gives us signs and obstacles in the way of things that are not meant for us. I also think the Universe will send you the right people who will help you on the path you need to follow.

How do I know? Because I've experienced it several times over. At first, I wasn't aware of what was going on. But there was a particular scenario where I consciously started to understand what was happening.

In 2021, mainly because of the pandemic, I moved from London to nearer where my parents lived so that I could see them more often. After all, who knew what was going to happen? I sold my flat, put an offer on a house not far from my parents, and was good to go. And then I moved in.

About two months later, it became clear this wasn't the house for me. The Universe sent me challenge after challenge (some that reduced me to anger and tears) until I had a moment of clarity. I didn't feel settled, and it didn't feel like home. I knew there was something better for me. I looked for other properties, but each one I enquired about was already sold, or there was a long waitlist to view it. I gave up looking.

But the Universe didn't give up. It knew I wasn't meant to be in this place. Something made me start looking for smaller, more luxurious properties. As you might imagine, they were few and far between. I don't know why, but one week

I made a real effort to start looking; there was a real drive in me. My brother-in-law sent me a property listing, but I thought it was out of my budget. Out of curiosity, I spoke to my mortgage company and learned it was within my reach. I booked a viewing for that property and another one nearby that wasn't as great.

I quickly realised what the Universe was up to on the day of the viewings. It was playing with me. I was to view the 'not really wanted' flat first. The bus app on my phone told me that my bus was cancelled, which happened between the time I left my house and walked to the bus stop, making me late (Sign #1). I had to walk fifteen minutes into town to be able to get another bus, and as I was doing so, my original bus sped past me!

So, I got to town and waited at the bus stop. One came along, but as I reached into my pocket to get my purse, my lip balm fell out and rolled away. The bus was about to leave, but I managed to wave to the driver to stop again (Sign #2). The Universe didn't want me to see this flat. I viewed it anyway, and as soon as I walked in, I knew it wasn't for me.

Then I went to see the next flat — the one the Universe wanted me to have. It immediately felt like home. Have you ever been in a situation where you instantly felt a sense of peace? That's how it was. The owner was lovely. We spoke for nearly an hour, and this place was perfect for what I wanted at that moment.

It was a stepping stone in the creation of my life — but I didn't let myself get excited. I was trying to play it cool, something I hadn't done before. A few days later, my offer was accepted. I'm editing this book from that flat now.

As if the signs I'd already received weren't enough to convince me I was following the right path, it all fell into place when I sold my home. In December 2021, I still hadn't decided whether to sell my current home or keep it and rent it out. I felt guilty that I hadn't spent even six months there! But I put the house up for sale in January 2022 and accepted an offer for the asking price within a week (Sign #3). That house was only meant for me for a short period of time.

When I initially moved from London, it was a bit of a rush decision due to not allowing myself a great deal of time to look for something. When I went to view the flat I'm now in, the seller told me he had put the flat up for sale in May of the previous year, just one week after I had put an offer on the house I had moved into! That sale fell through, fortunately for me, because it became available again when I decided to start looking again. Not listening to my Soul had taken me on a little detour, but in the end, it took me to exactly where I needed to be.

I want you to reflect on some of the big decisions you have made in your life — perhaps when you've moved home or country, taken a job, or ended a relationship. Ask yourself the following questions. Be honest with yourself.

1. What was the last decision you made that significantly improved your life?

2. How did you come to that decision? Did others suggest it? Was it intuition? Was it something that came out of the blue, and you knew you had to do it?

59

3. What was the last decision you made that did *not* improve your life, making it more stressful, with 'bad' things happening?

4. How did you come to that decision? Did others suggest it? Was it intuition? Was it something that came out of the blue, and you knew you had to do it?

LISTEN TO YOUR SOUL

It's not always enough to know there's a Treasure Chest for each of us. And it's easy to become frustrated, stuck, or resentful about things not going our way that we can ask ourselves why we're even here.

Sounds dramatic, right? But the truth is we do ask ourselves this in moments of extreme frustration or resentment. The feeling usually passes, but it isn't long before it's back again, and we're repeating the same questions.

It all comes back to the life we've been leading, the one that society, family, and friends have helped steer us towards. It's not a life of our creation or one that the Universe or our Soul wants us to live. Instead, it's a life of obligation. One where we 'have' to go to work. One where we 'have' to go to family gatherings, put on a brave face, or attend that work function or friend's event — even when we don't want to.

We tie up much of our worth in job titles, family positions, social connections, and education. We struggle in these roles when they don't feel right anymore, or when we remain in situations our Soul is no longer willing to accept. We flounder because we're growing a little at a time internally. And something we were happy with before suddenly doesn't interest or benefit us anymore.

I want to point out that not everyone struggles. Many people are more than content with the life they have. They either don't want to or feel they don't need to reflect on their life or themselves and change in any way. They're in a comfortable zone and are quite happy to stay there. And that is acceptable to them.

But if you're reading this book, I'm guessing you're struggling with some aspect of your life and seeking a change. Is there a nagging voice in your mind telling you there is something else? If so, I'm familiar with this voice, reiterating that you deserve more — the voice that keeps telling you something else is out there for you and invites you to keep looking and questioning.

Guess what? This is the voice of your Soul. And it won't stop talking to you until you choose to listen.

Have you ever tried to change things up in your life, but nothing seems to be working, and you're stuck in the same situations? Have you ever thought, 'Well, this must be it for me then because nothing is changing?' You may have read or heard the quote:

'It's not happening to you; it's happening for you.'

Even though you may feel you're not making any progress, I'm going to tell you that the Universe isn't done with you yet. Keep pursuing your dreams, and keep making changes, however small. Keep pushing because you *will* get to where you want to be.

Do you want to know how I know?

There have been many times in my life when I asked myself, 'Why am I here?', 'What is this particular situation giving me?', or 'How is it improving my life?' In most instances, the answer was a resounding 'It's not giving me anything. It's not improving my life.'

But the thing was, there was no one around me showing me anything different from what I already knew. Everyone was doing the same things, but they all seemed to feel much better in their lives than I was. Or, that was the impression I got.

When I was diagnosed with clinical depression in 2002, all those years ago, I was advised by my doctor to meditate and get in touch with my spirituality. He told me that doing so would alleviate many of my symptoms and bring me the peace my mind sought.

Like an obedient schoolchild, I did my research and started to meditate and bring spiritual practices into my life. At the time, these tools were not mainstream and were still considered a bit 'woo-woo.' I was lucky to find a meditation group that met once a week, but the collective energy and what I felt and saw freaked me out so much that I only attended twice. I turned to books to learn how to meditate and quiet the negative and sometimes scary thoughts going through my mind.

My experience with the meditation group, and then later in life learning about energies, made me realise that it is worth looking for a meditation teacher to begin with, or using one of the many apps available for your phone.

Practising meditation brought me a sense of comfort and peace. But once I felt 'fixed,' I discarded these tools, and I didn't think I needed them anymore.

Fast forward fifteen years later, when I was living in London. As I wrote about in the Introduction, I dropped into another nasty depressive episode that invited its friend anxiety to the party. This time, though, I had a lot more to lose. Over that period, I'd managed to find myself a stable and well-paid corporate job. I'd moved out of home into a rented flat in South London. I felt like I was in a good place for the first time. I was more social than I had been before. I was doing well at work, and I was enjoying my life.

This depressive episode hit harder because I wasn't expecting it. I started having panic attacks, especially after going out drinking. And not only did I have to deal with hangovers, but the panic attacks made everything ten times worse. It took a few years to realise that my self-abuse and toxic behaviour were my efforts to numb how I felt. I felt lost in the world. I didn't feel happy or satisfied with my life, even though I looked like I had it all together.

I committed again to therapy and found a fantastic therapist who helped set me on a better path for myself. I managed to get back on the other side of depression and anxiety, and I told myself (and unknowingly, the Universe) that I did *not* want to go through that again.

I fully believe that the Universe always listens to our thoughts — all the things we worry, dream, and hope about. Whatever we tell the Universe, it will provide. I told the Universe I didn't want to go through this experience again, and it responded. It helped me find a better way.

It wasn't long before meditation returned to my life, reconnecting me to my spirituality and leading me to practising yoga. I felt the same peace I'd felt before, but this time, I didn't discard these tools as soon as I felt better. I knew I wanted to keep them around so I could feel like this all the time, not just when I felt I needed it or when I was going through a bad patch. Even though I'd veered off the path I was meant to be on and taken quite the detour, I was led back to where my Soul needed to be.

It doesn't matter if you make a choice that takes you off your path. That detour may be needed for you to experience certain situations and learn specific lessons so that when you return to your path, it makes more sense and you feel less resistance.

I've had numerous moments in the past few years where I've suddenly realised that the 'detours' I took were much needed for my journey. I don't regret anything, not even my bouts with mental illness. Every moment, experience, the ups and downs, has led me to a life I've been creating with the Universe's help. And I wish this same life for you.

1. Have you experienced moments in your life when you made a decision that led you away from what you wanted? What happened?

2. Did you ever find your way back to the original decision you wanted to make? How did you get there?

FINAL THOUGHT

Everything you want in life is already available to you. It's just that you haven't been allowing your Soul to direct and guide you towards it. Now that you know you have this within your reach, it's time to listen to your Soul, take action by dreaming BIG, and make your Treasure Chest a reality.

CHAPTER THREE:
IT REALLY IS ALL ABOUT YOU

The moment you take responsibility for everything in your life, is the moment you can change anything in your life.

— Hal Elrod

IT REALLY IS all about you, you know. Does it feel natural to think of it that way, or do you think you need to keep putting others first? That is the selfless, giving way, after all. So, now that you know your dream life is within reach, how do you get it? I suggest the answer lies in focusing solely on yourself. Only others can change themselves, and only you can change yourself. We'll look at three key areas that drive this idea home:

- Take personal responsibility

- Realise only you can save yourself

- Accept that not everyone can join you on your journey

IT'S YOUR RESPONSIBILITY

Let's begin with personal responsibility. When I was in my thirties and deep in depression, I was very good at blaming the world for the bad situations I'd gone through. I never looked in the mirror and thought I had a part to play in all the things that happened in my life. Taking responsibility helped me become aware of how my behaviours, feelings, and actions played out in every aspect of my life.

Sure, we may be unable to control certain situations, especially when we are children. But when we reach adulthood, no one has responsibility for us — and we can't keep blaming others. We alone are responsible for how we show up in the world and react to situations and events in our lives. Saving yourself means taking responsibility for your life. Everything you consume, everything you do, everything you learn comes down to you.

I believe this point of taking responsibility for your life begins in your mid-twenties. By that age, if you're still creating destructive patterns and unnecessary situations that aren't helping you, that is negligence. You are still allowing society, family, and friends to be responsible for your life. And all the time you do that, you will never have the great life you dream of. You have to start putting things in place that will help you to live the life your Soul is here to live. Only your Soul can tell you that, not the people around you.

Though this may seem like a simple concept, plenty of people don't accept this responsibility. I've seen people old enough to know better still looking for someone else to take responsibility for them and what happens in their lives. And those people are the ones who, like my younger self, will not look in the mirror and ask themselves if they have a hand in their lives being the way they are.

Think about it. If you ask a successful or wealthy person who is responsible for them getting to that point, they will tell you it was down to them, their hard work, their connections, and the people who work for them. They would never say it was entirely down to someone else who got them there. But ask someone why they think their life isn't evolving as expected. More often than not, their answer will shift the blame to a suitable scapegoat — whether that's people or circumstances.

I remember an ex-colleague who was constantly negative about their life. They complained about relationships, jobs, health, and even people they didn't know. I wasn't always in a positive frame of mind at the time, but I was incredulous at the negativity this person felt. I often tried to help them reframe their thoughts but was met with more anger and frustration. They were not in a place to receive that help or advice. It was much easier for them to keep blaming external factors rather than reflect on how their actions or responses may have led to their unhappiness.

I recently listened to the *Diary of a CEO* podcast hosted by Social Chain founder/CEO Steven Bartlett. His guest, entrepreneur and author Mo Gawdat, has devoted much time researching what makes people happy, which he chronicles in his book, *Solve for Happy*. He spoke about happiness being a choice, noting that 8% of people would likely switch off the podcast on hearing that. That's because people don't want to hear they're responsible for their own happiness.

It's easier for some to believe that happiness comes from outside of us, in what we buy, our relationships, and what we consume. But it isn't; it comes from *inside* of us. We alone must choose to be content. And we can only do this once we take responsibility, acknowledge, and let go of the things that may have made our life more difficult than we wanted.

The same is true of the life you create. You are the co-creator with the Universe. If you continually think of negative situations or bad outcomes, you're sending a message to the Universe that you are willing to accept those situations and outcomes. And, in fact, you are asking for more of them.

If you think about more positive situations and abundant outcomes, the Universe receives the message that you want more of them. And it will happily oblige you. Your life is your choice, and your choices are your life.

NO ONE IS COMING TO SAVE YOU

We've established that only you have responsibility for yourself. As I've already mentioned, some people are happy to pass this responsibility to others, especially if that means they don't have to exert any effort into doing things. If they can just turn up and enjoy themselves, be taken care of, or have their name added as a contributor to a project, great!

But this kind of thinking and behaving leaks into other areas of life. It shows up in jobs, friendships, and our relationship with ourselves. It appears when we are unhappy about our life — because there is an unconscious belief that someone else will make everything okay and save us from the life we no longer enjoy.

Here's what you need to know: No one is going to save you. YOU have to save yourself. But first, you must realise you need saving and can't continue to carry on as you are.

The job you keep snoozing your alarm for every day won't get better unless YOU take responsibility and do something about what's bothering you. Maybe you're overwhelmed with your workload or are struggling with a colleague who isn't respecting you and your time. Others may be able to see what is happening, but they aren't going to fix the problems for you. They will likely turn a blind eye if it does not directly affect them — and they probably won't offer you advice. I've tried to help others with a particular issue but trying to help them find a solution only goes so far. They still had to take action. They had to save themselves. I couldn't do it for them.

I used to think I had to save everyone around me, that as the eldest child, everyone else was my responsibility, whether that was my grandparents, parents, or siblings. I believed I had to fix people from the pain and suffering they were going through. It wasn't until 2021 that I had the breakthrough that just as I can't expect others to save me, I'm not here to do that for others.

I was already in the process of saving myself and doing the work to put me on a better path. Because I was seeing benefits and feeling joyful and content, I wanted my family and friends to feel like that too. It made me sad to see people I loved still hurting and suffering, but I knew they had to save *themselves*.

When I've expressed to other people that I am not here to save them, they have seemed shocked. We like to play the hero in people's stories and be the one who changes their life or helps them overcome their struggles. This is natural because we want to feel needed by others.

In Chapter 8, I detail how I spent years trying to be the hero for someone financially. Not only did I lend them money, but I also tried to help them budget and understand why they couldn't financially support themselves despite being on a good wage. They never wanted to acknowledge that their financial mess was due to their actions and choices. They were happy to continue spending money on holidays and going out, wondering why they couldn't pay rent. Once I finally acknowledged I couldn't help them, I had to step away.

I'm not saying you should never help others when they are struggling. Just make sure you're in a place to help them. If you're not, you can feel resentment and frustration and even damage relationships when the other person doesn't start to see where they need to make changes or improve the situation themselves. I no longer talk to that person I tried to help, and I learned a tough lesson along the way. But it hasn't stopped me from helping others; I'm just more aware and make it clear how I will show up for someone.

NOT EVERYONE CAN COME ALONG

Just as I realised that I can't save others, I also learned I can't make people go on a particular journey. They have to do that for themselves. All I can do is embark on my own journey and hopefully inspire others to follow suit.

When I started on the path to the life I wanted to live, there were times when I felt so much joy and happiness that I wanted everyone else to feel the same. I wanted my family to see how much better life could be. I wanted my friends to see they didn't have to be stuck in the same situations for the rest of their lives.

Think about a time when you started something new, maybe a fitness routine, a health plan, or some type of study. When you were doing those things and making those changes to your life, I can guarantee that you felt accomplishment, contentment, and satisfaction — because you were moving your life forward. You weren't staying in the same place and letting life happen around you. You were the one taking control and making things happen. How many people did you try to recruit along the way? And did you manage to do that?

Think about when the roles are reversed. Have you ever been advised to make a change in your life? How did you feel about that? You may not have been as eager as the person suggesting it! It goes both ways.

As I was approaching forty, most people I interacted with were very into physical appearance and fitness. And I, being in a validation-seeking part of my life, was heavily influenced by this. I understood the need to keep my body moving and healthy. I enjoyed going to the gym, and after seeing and feeling these changes in my body, I naturally wanted everyone around me to feel the same.

I started talking more about what I was doing. I wanted everyone to realise that their health and fitness were important. But not many people listened, and I received many eye rolls. How could they not see how this would be of benefit to them? How could they not understand that other areas of their life would also improve? I was trying to be a hero. I was trying to save them from a life of feeling lethargic, unhealthy, and immobile.

That's not the first time I've done this. But something changed when I started to practice yoga and do more inner work. My yoga practice further solidified that this inner work can only be done by the person who will benefit from it. It can't be forced or encouraged, especially to those who are not ready or willing.

Making changes is about *us*, not about other people. Yes, others around us may benefit in some way because we have changed. If we put in boundaries at work and make sure we log off by a specific time, it's natural that our families will benefit from having us around a little more. If we decide to cut back on our drinking, others around us will benefit from us being more focused, less angry, or irritable.

The work I've done over the past few years has changed my life. I used to not understand why my loved ones didn't seem excited to join me. This was something I was coached on. I was sad I might lose those people close to me, but my coach asked, 'How do you know that they are not on their own journey?' I had been assuming their journey had to look exactly like mine!

I realised I'm not here to save them. All I can do is improve my life. When people around me see that I'm happier and more at ease, I hope it inspires them to get curious and do the same. That's when they will start to walk their own path. That's when they will see that creating their life is in their hands. It won't get handed to them. They will have to reach out and grab it.

The same holds true for you. Are you ready to reach out and grab the life that's meant to be yours?

Think of someone in your life who, in your eyes, is successful or seems to have their life together. This person doesn't have to be part of your inner circle but someone you have access to. It could be a parent at your child's school, a colleague, or someone in an exercise class you attend.

Now comes the hard part. Ask that person what they do to make their life 'successful.' There is a possibility of outcomes here:

1. They are flattered and share what they do.

2. They tell you they really don't have it all together.

3. They will run in the other direction.

Let's hope it's outcome #1!

What did you learn from this exercise? Were you surprised by what they told you, or was it something you had a feeling about all along? Record your answers below.

DAILY RITUALS AND GRATITUDE PRACTICE

I did the prior exercise when I started to intentionally create my life. I considered my mentors and people I followed on social media — not necessarily celebrities but people whose ethos I admired. And then I researched.

I either asked them or found out how they got to where they were and how they organised their lives to live how they wanted. I listened to podcasts and read books by people I respected to learn how they became and continued to be successful in their life.

When doing my research, I quickly learned that almost every one of these individuals took time in the morning or evening for reflection, spiritual practices, moving their bodies, and other grounding activities. Whatever daily ritual(s) they chose seemed to provide a store of energy for their day or recharged them at the end of the day. And they engaged in these rituals every day without fail.

Later in this book, I talk more about the daily practices that helped me to find a starting place. I was already meditating as part of my yoga practice, so it was one of the first and easiest things to build my morning routine around.

My research also revealed that all these people engaged in a daily gratitude practice. No matter how successful they had become, they still took time to express thanks for the blessings life had given them. They either wrote in a journal what they were thankful for or intentionally spoke or meditated on the words. This was the one practice that kick-started things for me when I deliberately set out to create a life I loved.

Before we can start to think about how we change our lives and get to the life we dream of, I believe it is important to be intentionally grateful

81

for everything we have created and experienced in our life so far. I don't have the words to express my thankfulness for this practice and how it has changed my mindset and life.

We can be very blasé and say, 'Of course, I'm grateful for everything in my life.' But have you ever intentionally expressed gratitude for your life and what you have? You may wonder why I keep using the word 'intentionally.' Taking time to purposely speak out or write down the things you are grateful for signals to the Universe your thankfulness for sending it your way. The Universe receives that signal and sends further blessings into your life. The more you express your gratitude, the more good things start to arrive and happen in your life.

I practice gratitude every day. Intentionally. It's not just a thought in my mind, but I choose to physically write down three things I am grateful for each morning. Some people speak their gratitude into existence, and I'm sure some people intentionally hold that gratitude in their hearts or minds — but writing down what I'm grateful for has made the most impact for me. It allows me to be creative with my words and reflect on what I want to express. It's always important to practice in a way that feels good for you; otherwise, it can feel like a chore.

I don't express gratitude only for positive things. I've been genuinely thankful for some unfortunate things in my life, even if I was initially angry, frustrated, and resentful. It wasn't until later (sometimes much later!) that I saw the blessing in what had happened.

It's okay not to feel gratitude for something the moment it occurs. Sometimes you won't see or feel gratitude for an event until long after it has happened. And one day, a light switch will be flipped in your head, and you will remember that situation and think about what may have been — and it will lead you to realise that you are in a much better place now.

I invite you to practise gratitude for seven days. Before starting the seven days, note how you are feeling. After the seven days, I want you to observe how you're feeling again. Choose your own way to practice: journal, meditate, speak your gratitude out loud, or whatever works for you.

1. What did you notice during the week?

2. How did you react to adverse situations?

3. How did you react to positive situations?

4. How was your perspective different during and after the exercise?

When I started practising gratitude, I thought I had to think 'big,' but the more I practised, the more I felt grateful for the small things in life:

Having working Internet;

Being able to buy food without having to think about a budget;

My bus to work arriving early.

Even little things started to build up the vibration I was sending out to the world. I became calmer in my life, and my tolerance for toxic behaviour drastically decreased. I'm easy-going and tend to get along with most people, and in the past, that has meant I've tolerated bad behaviour because it would cause too many ripples if I didn't. Gratitude helped me stick up for myself, and I found it easier to voice my opinions when I disagreed with things being said or done. And I wasn't worried about the approval from others because my own approval was more important.

COMPARISON IS THE THIEF OF JOY

Have you ever done something in the name of personal growth or self-improvement because someone else was doing it, claiming it 'changed their life?' If yes, was it something that genuinely lit you up, or was it something you thought would be a good idea because it would get you out of the 'stuck in a rut' feeling you'd been having? Did these activities enhance your life, or did they just make you feel even more dejected than before?

Or, how many times have you called your mum, only for her to tell you that a former classmate or distant relative is now married and moving abroad to live with her financier husband in Dubai? Just me? Okay, maybe the exact situation is different, but you get the idea.

When we start deliberately creating our lives, it's tempting to look at how others live theirs. We scrutinise other people's relationships, seemingly perfect families, jobs and careers, and even the activities they do in their free time. Observing others for inspiration for how we can enhance our lives is fine, but we must tread carefully.

Paying too much attention to the specifics can leave us open to comparing what we are doing with those around us. Rather than finding value in the inspiration, we can quickly assume we should be doing the same things others are doing.

We strive to be the same as these people because we think that is what a successful life looks like. And then we end up feeling those familiar emotions of being tired, burnt out, and frustrated because our life isn't how we want it to be. Comparing ourselves can bring us a great deal of stress and unhappiness. Instead, we must look at what *we* want and how *we* fit that into our lives to make it the best life for us.

I must admit I spent much of my life comparing myself and my life to others. Growing up in a Sikh family and Punjabi culture meant there was always someone getting married, having a baby, or getting a job promotion. And I always got to hear about it. Sometimes it didn't bother me, but there were times, especially as I got older (and of marrying age), that it did. No matter how many guys I was introduced to, none of them wanted to marry me. I remember how I would try to come across as the type of wife many Punjabi mothers wanted for their sons: someone who could cook and clean, look after the house, and have babies.

In their eyes, my employment didn't matter because I'd be expected to leave my job and move to where my husband lived. My education level didn't matter because I would be busy bearing and raising the future generation. It didn't matter how much I tried to be the person they wanted. I never seemed to measure up, which led me to compare myself to the young women who *were* getting married.

My comparisons with others didn't stop there. When I started work, I couldn't help comparing why I wasn't paid as much as others. Why wasn't I encouraged to train further to increase my chances of a promotion?

And then there was my social circle. I never felt like I fitted in with people. In my late teens and early twenties, I wanted to explore something other than family life, but I rarely was allowed to go out with friends due to my upbringing. Or, I'd have to answer so many questions to get my parents' permission that I often didn't bother to ask. It was easier to stay home and make excuses to my friends about why I couldn't join them. My friends from similar backgrounds would lie to their parents, but this never crossed my mind. I hadn't been raised to lie to my parents, and it was easier not to go out than to lie to them. But this stopped me from making any real connections growing up.

As a result, I rarely felt like I had a best friend or a group of friends to support me. I did socialise with people I met through college or work, but because I changed jobs quite often, I didn't have much stability in those friendships. I felt envious of groups of friends who had known each other for years and seemed to share the important milestones in life.

This comparison only kept me in the frame of mind of 'not being enough,' whether it be friendship, relationships, or my career. This comparison continued until I finally looked at myself rather than everyone and everything outside of me. When I turned inward and understood that comparing myself wasn't making me happy (no shit, Sherlock!) and looked at myself and my behaviour, my life finally started to change. Life became more manageable, and I was no longer finding resistance.

I began to attract better things to myself — friends, jobs, and opportunities that helped me grow — and started creating my life rather than 'copying' the life of other people. I realised there were certain things I had been doing for years that held no interest to me. I'd given them a go because they made other people happy, but because they weren't what my Soul wanted, these things only provided short-term joy and long-term disappointment.

FINAL THOUGHT

When you are in the process of creating your life, it is easy to rush it and take on the things that other people enjoy. Remember to turn inward and ask yourself whether this activity, environment, person, situation, or opportunity is what *you* want. Take your time and remember to keep listening to your Soul, for it will always be guiding you towards your greatest good.

CHAPTER FOUR:

YOUR HIGHER SELF FOR YOUR GREATEST GOOD

Your Higher Self is whispering softly in the silence between your thoughts.

— Deepak Chopra

A S WE'VE ADDRESSED the Soul in Part 1, we've covered how to take actionable, realistic steps to move beyond your limiting beliefs

(Chapter 1), access your Treasure Chest (Chapter 2) by learning to listen to your Soul's voice, and take responsibility for your journey (Chapter 3).

We'll round out Part 1 by getting into the *woo-woo* in this and the next chapter. And I say *woo-woo* because the ideas I'm going to put forward may not resonate with some people, and they can seem alien and a bit 'out there.' In actuality, these ideas are nothing new; they've been around for centuries in various forms and guises in different religions and spiritual practices.

So, let's begin: You are not on this journey alone. Someone else is always on this journey with you, someone very important — and that is your Higher Self.

Your Higher Self is THE BEST, MOST FULLY EXPRESSED VERSION OF YOU. It is the version of you enjoying all the fruits of your Treasure Chest while you are struggling or waiting to reach that place. It is the version of you that already knows the path you need to tread and how to navigate that path. It knows what decisions you will make to get to where you need to be, and it is the version of you that has already met people you haven't even heard of yet. But that version of you is still YOU. And when we create the life we want to live, our Higher Self is the person we want to be.

A short note on your Higher Self and your Soul: They are not the same, so please don't berate yourself if you feel confused. Your Soul holds your desires and dreams, and your Higher Self can be considered the instrument to bring those desires and dreams to life. Your Higher Self is the logical, practical part of you that helps you to create behaviours and situations for your desires and dreams to become real.

Are you ready to meet *your* Higher Self?

VISUALISING YOUR HIGHER SELF

I want you to do a short visualisation. Read through the visualisation before you begin. Close your eyes and take a few deep breaths. Now think about your life three to five years from now:

1. Where are you?

2. What are you wearing?

3. What are you doing?

4. Who are you with?

5. What are you feeling?

Use your five senses to keep the visualisation as authentic as possible:

1. What do you see?

2. What do you smell?

3. What do you hear?

4. What can you touch?

5. What can you taste?

Sit here as long as you need to, drinking in all the information in this visualisation. When ready, take a few deep breaths and return to the present. I want you to write down everything you can remember from this visualisation below. This is the vision your Higher Self wants you to see and remember. This is the version of you that you know you will become.

It can be challenging to visualise ourselves in the future because we are so concerned with what we need to do in the present moment — our chores, other people's demands, and our jobs. But doing so gives us the motivation to keep growing and moving forward.

I took part in this visualisation during a group coaching session. It wasn't something I had done before. Going through the specific steps, dropping into my heart, and allowing myself to see the future was very emotional. It brought me to tears because I'd never seen myself this way. This visualisation introduced me to my Higher Self. I always knew she existed, but I had never met her until that day. And the warmth and happiness I felt in that visualisation motivated me to continue to grow to become her and work towards the life she had shown me.

Each of us wants to be better tomorrow than we are today. We want to be less angry, less resentful, and less frustrated. We want to be more joyful, more optimistic, and full of more lightness and energy. The best way to try and do this is to become the highest version of ourselves. Because that person is the one who has the qualities and life that we are looking for.

When I was in the depths of depression, I wasn't what I would classify as a nice person. I was angry a lot of the time, and I had a lot of negative and self-defeating thoughts. There were many times when I thought I would never be happy again — and many times when I wondered what the point of my life was. But somewhere deep down, I knew there had to be another way. Surely life wasn't always going to be like this. There had to be a life where dark thoughts and emotions weren't the only thoughts I had or the emotions I felt.

I didn't know how to get to that life, and it took me a long time to understand how to get there. It's something I've intentionally set myself on the path to do in the last few years. Before that, everything was a half-hearted attempt at making my life better for myself. I did the things I read about in magazines or heard others speak about, like going for spa days, connecting with people, and training for jobs I didn't feel passionate about.

As I now know, the Universe still gave me challenges and tried to show me the path for me, but I took little notice. And so it took me a little longer (in my mind) to get to where I wanted to be. But everything in life happens at the exact time it is supposed to take place. We do not get to a place and point in time until we are ready to experience what that place and point in time has for us.

HOW TO TAP INTO YOUR HIGHER SELF

Your Higher Self is always with you. Many of us don't acknowledge this part of ourselves because we concentrate so much on what we are in the here and now. We do not reflect or vision cast, so we cannot see lessons or opportunities that can bring us to the best version of ourselves.

Your Higher Self, with a bit of help from the Universe, is the part of you that guides you without you knowing. Have you ever had a situation where you've been inexplicably drawn towards a particular outcome over a different one? You could call it a gut feeling or your intuition kicking in. Or have you had an intense feeling about choosing one thing over another? Maybe you drove a different route to a familiar destination because you felt drawn to that and later found out that a traffic build-up would've made you late to where you were going. That's your Higher Self looking out for you, guiding you.

Have you ever asked for guidance in a situation to have a voice in your head give you the answer you need? That's your Higher Self directing you.

Tapping into your Higher Self is one of the most beneficial ways to create your life because they already know what your 'perfect' life looks like. They are best placed to lead you through the creation of that life.

So how do you get closer to your Higher Self? How do you tap into the benefits? You've already done a visualisation to meet your Higher Self, but how can you continue to tap into their knowledge?

We'll look at three practices to become more acquainted with your Higher Self:

1. Meditation

2. Journalling

3. Oracle Cards

Meditation

Meditation is one of my favourite ways of contacting my Higher Self if I want guidance or reassurance. I find a quiet spot and slowly bring myself into a meditative state. From here, once I feel comfortable, I will greet my Higher Self before asking questions I already know I want to ask or questions that come into my mind. Responses aren't always immediate, and there have been times when I've been unable to tap in.

If you want to try this method, find a quiet spot where you won't be disturbed. Get comfortable, close your eyes, and inhale and exhale deeply a few times. I also encourage you to get to know your Higher Self before asking for guidance. Spend a few sessions getting to know them. You will know you're ready once you feel comfortable enough to start working with your Higher Self more intentionally.

I always greet my Higher Self; after all, I would be rude to launch into a list of questions without acknowledging that they are there! Take time to welcome your Higher Self. Imagine you're on a coffee date and going for a chat with your best friend. Ask the questions out loud or in your head when it feels right. Wait for your Higher Self to respond. Don't be downhearted if you don't get a response or if it takes a while to come through. It can sometimes take a few attempts before you start to see results. The more you work with your Higher Self or just talk through things, the easier this becomes. This is because you are tapping into the part of you that is usually pushed to one side as you go through life.

Journalling

Journalling is another excellent way to tap into your Higher Self. Write out questions and let your Higher Self channel what they want to say through responding.

This isn't someone else taking control of your pen, but rather it is letting the energy of your Higher Self flow through the pen so that you write down what your Higher Self wants you to know or do. This is similar to inner child work, where you write down questions and allow your inner child to speak through the writing.

When I use this method, I like to light a candle, grab a few crystals (depending on what type of conversation I want), and do a short meditation before I start. And remember, this is the creation of your life, so you can set yourself up in whatever way you want. You might like to do this first thing in the morning or last thing at night. Or, you may want to listen to music to evoke a specific emotion or make yourself a cup of tea before sitting down to write. Do what makes you feel comfortable.

Oracle Cards

Oracle cards are another favourite way to access my Higher Self. It's especially good if I want quick guidance. I have several Oracle decks that I like to use, and I've listed these in the Resources section.

Before pulling a card, I like to take a few moments to ground myself and enter a receptive state. I've usually got a question in mind, so I hold the deck, close my eyes, and ask my question. I then split the deck into two and whichever card is facing up is the guidance that I take. Sometimes I like to spread the cards out in a semi-circle and let myself be drawn to the one that will bring me advice.

It is a fun way to bring intuition into my life. I'm not the only one who has pulled a card and then realised either at that moment or later that day that my Higher Self was sending me an important message.

Over the next week(s), make some space and time to explore the three different methods of accessing your Higher Self.

To work with the meditation method:

1. Think about any situation or challenge you face now for which you want guidance.

2. Tap into your Higher Self by finding a comfortable place to be silent and focused.

3. Greet your Higher Self.

4. Ask your Higher Self for guidance on your identified situation or challenge.

5. Take your time to listen.

6. Absorb any words or visions that come to mind.

7. Thank your Higher Self.

8. Come back to the present. If it helps, write down what you heard or saw.

To work with the journalling method:

1. Think about any situation or challenge you face now for which you want guidance.

2. Tap into your Higher Self by finding a comfortable place to be silent and focused.

3. Greet your Higher Self.

4. Ask your Higher Self for guidance on your identified situation or challenge.

5. Let yourself write whatever comes to mind.

6. Thank your Higher Self.

7. Reflect on what you have written down.

For Oracle Card pulls, use the steps below:

1. Think about any situation or challenge you face now for which you want guidance.

2. Tap into your Higher Self by finding a comfortable place to be silent and focused.

3. Greet your Higher Self.

4. Ask your Higher Self for guidance on your identified situation or challenge.

5. Shuffle the cards and pick one card from random.

6. Read the accompanying message for the card.

7. Reflect on how the card made you feel when it was pulled and the message that goes along with it.

There have been times when I have gone through one or all of these processes, but nothing resonated with me. It didn't feel true to me, and sometimes it wasn't the answer I was looking for! This is perfectly okay. Sometimes the message we receive will not make sense straight away. It could be that day or weeks later when you realise what your Higher Self was trying to tell you. Don't be disheartened. The more you connect with your Higher Self, the easier this will become, and the messages you receive will resonate more.

[NOTE: I speak more about meditation, journalling, and oracle cards in Chapter 12.]

FINAL THOUGHT

Our Higher Self is an important piece of the puzzle for creating the life we want. We can't ignore that it already is the better, more improved version of ourselves. It can be powerful in leading us in the direction we need to go so that we get to the life of our dreams.

Checking in with our Higher Self is an easy and fun way of manifesting everything our Treasure Chest already holds for us.

CHAPTER FIVE:

DE-MYSTIFYING MANIFESTATION

What you think, you become. What you feel, you attract. What you imagine, you create.

— Buddha

MANIFESTATION. You may have heard this word thrown around a lot recently, as in manifesting a new relationship, a new car, a new home, or a job. There is a buzz around manifesting what you want in your life, but what does that mean?

If you look at the definition of manifestation in the *Oxford Learner's Dictionary*, it is 'an event, action, or thing that is a sign that something exists or is happening; the act of appearing as a sign that something exists or is happening,' such as riots happening due to the discontent of society.

Spiritually speaking, it means something different. Manifestation is using attraction and belief to bring something tangible into your life. It is about bringing the things that you dream about into your reality.

So how does manifestation work? Have you ever heard the saying, 'Be careful what you wish for?' When you put out an intention, vocally or not, you ask the Universe for this very thing. And for some of us, our thoughts err on the negative side. So when the Universe hears them, it thinks you want more of this.

Some of my mentors say that the Universe is one big YES button. Whatever you think of or ask for, the Universe responds with a big fat YES! If you think you are always attracting bad luck, the Universe will take that as a sign to bring you more bad luck. If you're always thinking about how miserable your job is, the Universe will take that as a sign to bring you more misery in your job. If you don't believe me, look at certain past situations in your life and explore how they played out.

When I was constantly thinking about the amount of debt I was in and not trying to think of ways to get out of the debt, the Universe sent me more opportunities to get deeper into debt. That was until I made the intention and declared I no longer wanted to be financially tied to paying off my debts for the rest of my life. As soon as I made that declaration, the Universe sent me opportunities to help myself out of that debt.

At a point, I realised that I had paid off all of my debt and was finally in a good financial position. I was so proud of myself because I hadn't been actively thinking about my debt all the time. Instead, I was making plans to improve my financial standing, taking the opportunities sent my way because the Universe knew I wanted to get out of debt.

Manifesting is not just about declaring what you want, sitting back, and hoping it will appear at your door. Remember from Chapter 4 that declaring and dreaming without taking action is just a wish! This is where people go wrong and then accuse the concept of manifestation of being spiritual nonsense.

Manifestation requires you to declare what you want *and* take action. You could express that you want a new relationship. Great, the Universe will get straight on it! Or so you think. If you haven't told the Universe what you want in that relationship or when you want these things, you could wait for the next twenty years for someone completely unsuitable! That brings me to...

GET SPECIFIC

Let's look at this new relationship you desire. If that is the extent of your declaration, the Universe will send new relationships your way. But how will you know it's the right one for you? You won't because you haven't been specific enough, and you haven't declared *when* you want this relationship to show up. You haven't disclosed this person's personality traits or how they should physically look. You haven't declared what type of work that person should be doing or how financially stable they are.

I could go on, but if you send out a vague message to the Universe, it will send back vague opportunities. When manifesting, you must hone in on what you want. What are your deal breakers and the areas where you will compromise? That helps to send out a more narrow message to the Universe so it can bring in exactly what you want.

Let's say you want a new job. The Universe could send you anything: retail jobs, hospitality jobs, medical jobs. But you know these are not the jobs you are after. You want something in leadership where you are designing training courses and helping people improve their career prospects. Unless you tell the Universe this, it won't know to send you the right opportunities. Is this starting to make sense?

If there is something I want to manifest for myself, I sit down with a piece of paper and write down exactly what I want. I also write down what I want to *feel* when I have this particular thing.

Recall the story I told in Chapter 2 about purchasing my second flat. When I decided to move, I wrote down everything I wanted in my new home. I was willing to compromise on some things but not on others. Except for a few small things, I got exactly what I asked for. And that leads into...

ALIGN WITH THE UNIVERSE

If you and the Universe are aligned, and you're following the signs and taking action, manifestation can happen very quickly — unless you've asked for it to hold off. The Universe will only give you what it knows you can handle at that moment. If you've asked for a promotion in your job — to manage a team, for example — but haven't spent time improving your management skills, the Universe will be wary about giving you what you want. Or it will provide you with what you want, and you'll face considerable challenges in your new role.

So what does being in alignment mean? It's not just about the sun, moon, and stars being in the right place at the right time to deliver something. It's also about YOU. You are a big piece of this puzzle. You already know the Universe will take notice of what you declare. It also observes the vibration or level you are playing at to determine when to deliver. Are you living at a high vibration, or are you still stuck in negative mindsets and beliefs about yourself and what you deserve in your life? If the Universe gave you what you wanted today, would you be able to handle it or more?

You may have realised that I love examples and stories. Say you put a declaration or intention into the Universe about your dream home. This dream home would cost you a pretty high price in terms of money, something you'd see in magazines, all high ceilings, lots of light, and a luxurious feel.

The Universe would get excited because it likes to have fun. But it notices that you're not allowing yourself to live luxuriously right now. It sees that you're still worrying about money, so it doesn't consider you a good match for this amazing home it has put aside for you. Because don't forget, this home is already in your Treasure Chest. You just haven't got it yet.

If you aren't in the correct mindset or don't let your body feel the sensation of living in this new home, the Universe cannot deliver. You will essentially block yourself from receiving this fantastic new house. And when you see that this house you dream about is not making its way to you, you get downhearted. You start to doubt whether you will ever get the things you want — leading to your dreams being put on hold or discarded. Many of us end up in this cycle, keeping us in the same place we are today.

We have to prepare ourselves to receive the things we want. We may need to change our mindset, break through limiting beliefs, or work on childhood patterns and trauma — all of which can block us from receiving the Universe's gifts.

It wants us to have our heart's desires, but we turn away at the first sign of 'failure.' Those things will still be there for us; someone else will not inherit them. But to receive them, we must be open, willing, and ready to receive them.

WHEN WE DON'T GET WHAT WE WANT

There are two reasons why we don't manifest what we want:

1. **We don't think we deserve the thing we are trying to manifest.** When we don't believe we deserve something, we block those things trying to come to us. We are already saying that we couldn't possibly accept what the Universe wants to give us.

2. **Something much better is waiting for us.** We want a certain thing, and we usually keep this to something realistic — because then we can be almost sure that we'll receive that thing. We don't let ourselves dream bigger. But the Universe knows what is for you. It knows what you deserve, so if it thinks that particular thing or wish is not enough for you, it won't grant it. The Universe will make you wait for the better thing. You may have heard the saying, 'Rejection is just redirection.' When you don't get what you want, don't be disheartened because there is something better in the works for you.

I remember applying for jobs in my early twenties when I was first looking for a full-time position. I wrote more than fifty letters to local accountants and accountancy firms because that's the industry I thought I wanted to work in at the time (cultural expectations played a big part in this). For every letter I wrote, I received a rejection. I'm not sure what kept me going and not giving up.

I finally decided to apply for other types of jobs, not just accountancy roles. Out of all the prospective letters I wrote, I received only one positive response for a job at a company where one of my uncles worked. I had avoided applying there because I was trying to step out of his shadow. I'd already followed his lead in the subjects I studied at college, but when I saw that I was not academically built for those subjects, I changed my educational course. I didn't want to follow his career choices and fail at those too.

Though I felt some resistance, I still applied for the job, and it wasn't long before I was interviewed, offered and accepted the position. Even though I had spent a great deal of time researching and writing to many accountancy firms, there was only one role meant for me at that time. And it was the role I least expected. I accepted the position and ended up learning a great deal about office dynamics and politics. I stayed there for around two years before I was headhunted by an insurance broking firm in London.

I had never heard about manifestation at the time and was oblivious to how the Universe worked. But since learning about it and seeing it in action, I now know to trust its signals. When certain things 'pop' into my head, I've learned to explore them in case there is something the Universe is trying to guide me towards.

When writing this book, I looked back at the jobs I applied for. Since those first fifty or so rejections, I have only ever been turned down for one role. Some may call that lucky, but I know that when I applied for those roles, they were the only role I applied for because they were the roles I wanted. I believed that I would be offered the job after an interview, and it happened every time except for one.

Since learning more about manifestation, I looked deeper at some of my jobs. For the last corporate role I took, I had planned to apply about four months before my start date, and I wanted to return to one of the previous companies where I had worked. The company had a great team that mutually respected each other, and my ex-colleagues there shared that positions were always available for the right people.

At the time, I'd also decided I wanted to work a four-day week because I wanted the flexibility to pursue other things, but I didn't want to lose out on finances. I knew the company was pretty flexible with their staff, so I applied. My previous managers invited me for an informal interview. A few days later, I accepted a position at this company, working only four days a week for more money than which I'd previously worked five days a week. (I write about this in more detail in the Introduction.)

I was so sure of getting the role that I hadn't applied for anything else. That was the role I wanted, and I could visualise myself back at the company working exactly how I wanted. And because I had given out strong, specific signals to the Universe and was ready, that's exactly what I received.

FINAL THOUGHT

Playing with manifestation is a great way to see where you are in life and whether you need to change your vibration in order to receive what you want. I love to experiment with manifestation, bringing a bit of magic into my daily life with crystals and oracle decks. Sometimes, though, it helps to ease into manifestation by utilising a more traditional tool such as writing out lists of what you want.

Looking Ahead

In Part 2, *The Practices*, we'll explore in Chapters 6 and 7 how the Wheel of Life gives us a 'birds-eye view' of the different areas of our life and identify where we want to devote more energy or cut back. Then, we'll address our financial health in Chapter 8. Consider these all as practical tools to provide a more methodical approach to manifestation.

PART TWO

CHAPTER SIX:

THE WHEEL OF LIFE (Part 1)

Don't wait for everything to be perfect before you decide to enjoy your life.

— Joyce Meyer

I'VE WRITTEN IN previous chapters about ideas I feel are more spiritual and linked to creating the life our Souls are here to live. In this and the next chapter, we'll look at one of the more practical and traditional tools I use with my clients to examine the current state of their lives: The Wheel of Life, also known as the Life Balance Wheel.

It can feel overwhelming when we talk about changing our lives to create a life we love. Many of us want to change everything all at once. I know you want it all — and there are authors, leaders, and gurus who will tell you that you can have it all. But I'm not here to tell you that. I prefer a dose of realism with my creativity!

Along with 'having it all,' a lot is spoken about balance in our lives, whether it is work, family, relationships, recreation, or self-development. I don't believe in balance — the idea of keeping every area of our life at the same level for a prolonged period. It's simply not sustainable. Life shifts daily, and I will discuss balance later in this chapter.

We often don't consider our lives as a whole when prioritising a specific area. When we change one area of our lives, we often hope that the rest of our lives will also miraculously change.

The Wheel of Life helps us identify the areas of our lives we want to prioritise so we can compromise or sacrifice more intentionally. When we start changing one aspect of our life, we'll inevitably cause this change to ripple into other areas.

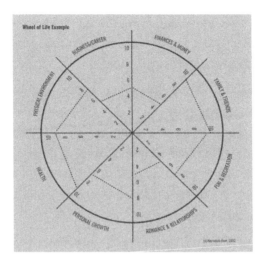

EXERCISE #1

The Wheel of Life highlights eight different areas of life and scores from 1 through 10 for each area. You can get a downloadable version at www.harmeschkaur.com that you can print out and complete or simply write out as a list.

With your Wheel of Life page and a pen or pencil, I want you to score each area of life represented on the wheel on a scale from 1 to 10 — with 1 being 'not very satisfied' and 10 being 'completely satisfied.' There are no right or wrong answers here; it is purely based on how you feel right now about different areas of your life.

Once you've completed this, you will be able to identify areas of life you wish to work on to increase your satisfaction levels. There may be areas that stick out immediately that you have known you wanted to work on all along, and there may be areas that surprise you.

When you have your list, put it into priority order according to which area of your life is most important for you. For example, even if you have a satisfaction score of 4 for Business/Career and a 6 for Health, you may now feel that your health warrants a higher priority for improvement than Business/Career does.

Please know this isn't a one-time exercise. Don't think that because you have these scores now and make priority calls on specific areas, this is it for the rest of your life! You can do this exercise as often as you want to because we go through various life stages, and different situations may give us different results. Doing the exercise will help you feel less overwhelmed and focused rather than thinking that your entire life needs an overhaul!

The Wheel of Life aims to give you direction and help you create goals and action plans for creating a life you love. And one other thing to remember here: I would not advise (and it's humanly impossible) to work on all areas of your life simultaneously. Picking one or two as a priority will shift your life more than you realise and can positively affect the areas you've placed at a lower priority. Don't try to do everything at once!

I like to do this exercise at the end of the year to plan my goals for the following year. I also review it mid-year to make sure I'm on track or identify whether I need to pivot my priorities. When I first did this exercise, Personal Growth was my most important area. But as my satisfaction with my Personal Growth improved, it also had a knock-on effect on Family/Friends and Fun/Recreation. So three areas of my life began to improve. Doing the exercise again helped me see that my Physical Environment needed attention, so I worked on this, which also impacted my Finances and Health.

I hope you can see that even when we put one area of our life as a priority for action and improvement, other areas of our lives benefit.

EXERCISE #2

In addition to completing your own Wheel of Life in the previous exercise, under each area, write down:

1. What do I like about this area of my life?

2. What do I dislike about this area of my life?

Keep these answers handy, as you'll need them in Chapter 7.

Now, I wouldn't blame you for feeling a bit overwhelmed. It's okay to feel this way, and please allow yourself the grace to sit with that. It means you are invested in personal change and want to move in a forward direction rather than going backwards or staying still. It means you are ready to change things in your life and go for the things you know you deserve.

IT'S ABOUT BALANCE...OR IS IT?

Life balance is a phrase I first heard in the late nineties. Years of partying and rushing through life left many people feeling burnt out and stressed out. The term 'wellness' started to appear more in the news and media but was touted as something only practised by those who were a bit 'hippy-ish.'

The last ten to fifteen years, however, have seen a boom in the wellness industry and we are all being encouraged to take time for ourselves and ensure we have balance in our life. But what does balance mean?

For many of us, it is really the balance between work and the rest of our lives. Because we spend so much time at work and getting paid to do things that don't truly matter to us, it leaves us with little time to do the things that do matter to us.

The Wheel of Life is designed to show our satisfaction in each of its eight areas, but it also shows how balanced we feel in each area. Unconsciously, we are not trying to achieve balance but are striving to be satisfied in all areas of our life.

When our relationships suffer because we give too much time and energy to work, we start to work on those relationships. That then throws out our fun and recreation time or our finances. And then work begins to suffer, so we focus on our jobs again. Where is the balance?

I'm sure you've heard the concept of spinning plates. They all start spinning, and then one slows down, so it has to be given attention. Then another one, and maybe one more until our attention is so fractured that the plates drop to the floor and smash, leaving us with little or nothing left to spin.

As I've stated earlier in this chapter, I believe there is no such thing as balance. I have been that person who has tried to live a 'balanced' life. I allocated time to each area of my life to achieve a sense of equilibrium. And there were times I felt I had it figured out. I tried to do everything: work, see family and friends, care for my health and fitness, save money, develop and improve myself, and pursue hobbies. And there were times when I felt all these areas and goals were being met.

Then I decided I wanted to move home (I write about this in detail in Chapter 2). I underestimated the time, energy, and tasks needed to do this one thing. It ended up taking over my life and pushing my other primary commitment at the time — my coaching business — to the side. My business was beginning to gain traction. I was building up my brand and audience, reaching out to clients, and seeing results. And then my new priority hit me like a ton of bricks.

I didn't know how to make space for my business and the move, and I quickly ran out of energy to keep those plates spinning (as well as my 9-to-5 job and everything else). The business plate fell, and I had to accept it. I then signed up for a four-month self-development course because why not add another plate to the mix! And that's when I learned there is no such thing as balance.

At different times in our lives, we will have different priorities and things we want to work on or focus on. But we need to allow ourselves the grace to realise that when that priority is being looked after, something else may have to end up lower on our list for a while. And that is not a bad thing.

We are taught to keep everything going (spinning our plates), so it doesn't feel natural to give ourselves permission to put something down for five minutes whilst we concentrate on something else. We don't step back to look at what will have the most significant impact on our life in this present moment — and then focus solely on that. We continue trying to keep everything going, which is impossible!

The four-month programme I was enrolled in (Stretch 22) had a module called 'The One Thing.' As you can probably imagine, this programme section had me explore the one thing that would have the most significant impact on my life and move me to where I wanted to be. This was the thing that deserved my attention and my energy. Everything else was sprinkles!

This book you're reading was my One Thing. I have wanted to write a book for more than twenty-five years. And I have. But I have been rejected over and over by agents and publishers, so I put my dream and writing to one side. I know now that the books I was writing were not my books to write; they were practice books.

But this one was my book to write.

I set standards around my writing: Five days a week, with a first draft done within six months. I worked out how many days there were in those six months if I allowed only five days per week, subtracting any days I knew I wouldn't write, such as Christmas or special occasions. I then worked out how many words I would have to write in total, and then each day.

I stuck to it — and now you're reading that book.

Sometimes I didn't write daily, but I didn't beat myself up. I let the process flow. But the most important thing was that I focused on the book. I made it a priority in my life. I had learned that something else in my life may need to take a back seat. For me, that started off as being sleep, fun, and recreation time.

But then a funny thing started to happen. Although I had 'sacrificed' other areas of my life to focus on my One Thing, time seemed to appear in my day to do the other things I wanted to focus on. I suddenly had pockets of time to devote to my coaching business and hobbies. Don't get me wrong, it wasn't always easy. I'd also decided halfway through to start waking up earlier each day to write. That gave me time at the other end of my day to do things that wouldn't take up so much of my mental energy.

Balance is fluid. One day, one thing may be your priority. The next day it may be something else. Something will always have to be sacrificed for you to focus on your priority. That is not bad, and we need to stop believing it is. Getting every area of your life to a 10 out of 10 will burn you out. If you let that balance be more fluid, you'll have more fun and enjoy the journey a lot more!

FINAL THOUGHT

The Wheel of Life is the perfect tool to get to a starting point before you begin making further changes in your life. In Chapter 7, we'll delve deeper to discover which areas you want to improve or make changes.

CHAPTER SEVEN:
THE WHEEL OF LIFE (PART 2)

True life is lived when tiny changes occur.

— Leo Tolstoy

LET'S ADDRESS each of the eight areas of the Wheel of Life in more detail.

I feel it's important for me to caveat that these are my views and opinions. I've drawn on my own experiences and of people I know. Many of these experiences come from my clients. You may not relate to some of the experiences here, and that's okay. We each have thoughts and ideas about our experiences and situations, and no one thing or person is right or wrong. I only ask that you keep an open mind. Take what resonates and leave anything that doesn't!

I've added a short exercise at the end of each section. You can complete these as you go through them, or you can wait until you've read the whole chapter and do them in one go. However you choose to do them, be honest with yourself. No one has to know how you feel or think about a particular area of your life. But *you* need to know so that you can start to work on what is important to you.

BUSINESS & CAREER

I've picked this area first because this is one of the areas that many of us often use to define ourselves in life. When we meet people, one of the first questions we are asked, or ask, is, 'What do you do?' Our job roles become a badge and can end up defining the path we take in life.

As I've gotten older and explored different life paths for myself, I've met more people living their passion rather than keeping a job that pays the bills. But once we have that badge or label, it can be challenging to remove it from ourselves and try to become something different. I worked as a Business Analyst for more than ten years. Most people don't have a clue what a Business Analyst is. I certainly didn't until I actually started doing the job! My mum always used to tell people I worked in a bank because it was easier to explain. And technically, I did work in a bank, just not in the way that people tend to perceive. I worked on technology projects, helping to improve how systems were used or implement new ones. Yes, exciting stuff!

I liked certain aspects of this work — using my analytical skills, working with people, drawing out answers to my many questions, and helping to shape solutions. But the end result of a new software system or business process didn't inspire me. There came a point in my life a few years ago when I knew I didn't want to work in this industry anymore, and especially in this type of role. But having done the work for so long, and like many other people in the same predicament, I didn't know *what* I wanted to do.

And that is the biggest hurdle for many of us when it comes to changing jobs or careers. We just don't know what we want to do — because we simply don't allow ourselves the time or space to explore and discover new avenues of work. That creates inertia because we don't allow ourselves to push any further to find out what we might actually want to do.

Most of us spend more than half of our waking moments at work. Unfortunately, this isn't constrained to those who work in corporate jobs or work for other people. It also applies to many people who work for themselves, especially in the trade industry. It makes sense for us to spend time doing something we love or feel brings value to the world.

There's another hurdle: Many of us have little self-belief that we can do something else and don't believe we *can* change our jobs. We don't have confidence in our abilities, or maybe one of the other areas of our lives is also getting in our way. And that's *before* we have those close to us telling us that we're crazy to think of changing our job situation in uncertain times. This is why it's essential to find out where our lives seem out of balance to correct that and work towards the life we love rather than merely exist.

Time for a question: If you could do or be anything in this world, what would it be? I'm giving you permission to dream really big here. A doctor or nurse? A human rights activist? A writer? An actor? All of these things (and many more) are possible. But as soon as we see the words or have the thought, the next immediate notion is, 'I can't do that.' This comes back to those beliefs placed on us by family, friends, and society. Just because *they* can't do it doesn't mean *you* can't.

I will keep saying it until you start to believe it: You are not the only person who feels like there's a better way for you. Many people in your town, country and the world aren't happy with their jobs. Yet, they will remain in those jobs until it's time to retire because that's the only door they see as leading to the start of the rest of their lives.

However, there is another door you can walk through that can come any time before retirement. It's actually preferable that it does because why would you wait until retirement to live the life you want? It's the self-discovery door. Choose to walk through it and start researching other passions and possible ways to earn an income. It simply comes down to priorities.

I'll give you two cautionary tales of missing priorities:

Cautionary Tale #1: Lost Initiative

I worked with an Australian company in 2019 on a one-year contract. One of my colleagues was one of the nicest and funniest guys I'd ever met.

He was intelligent and great at his job. Still, he didn't enjoy his career, and he didn't feel motivated — but it paid good money and gave him somewhat of the lifestyle he wanted. He didn't feel valued at work, but he didn't know what he wanted to do.

Seeing my friend struggle, I suggested he carve out time to research and explore different jobs and areas of work that *would* interest him. Did he do that? When I last checked LinkedIn, he was still in the same role — possibly still not enjoying his job. Do you want to look back in three or four years and wonder where the time went?

Cautionary Tale #2: Lost Time

About ten years ago, I thought of training as a nutritionist whilst working full-time in a job I didn't particularly enjoy. I'd become addicted to going to the gym and how to fuel my body. I was feeling great and wanted everyone else to feel the same way. But when I looked into getting a qualification, the minimum amount of time I had to spend studying was three or four years. I thought, 'That is too long to be spending studying and having to stay in this job.' So, I didn't pursue the qualification. Guess what? Those four years went by anyway, and I was still in that job with no qualifications. Time really doesn't hang about for any of us.

1. What do you enjoy doing in your current job?

2. What do you not enjoy about your current job?

3. What changes would you make about your current job to make it something you are happy to get out of bed for?

4. What would your dream job be?

5. What would it take to get your dream job? For example, would it mean studying for several years to change careers? Would it mean transferring to a different team at work?

PHYSICAL ENVIRONMENT

This section is all about where you are living. Aside from our work environments, I'm referring to your physical environment as the place we spend the most time. It's important that our environment is nurturing us, providing comfort and a safe place from other stresses in our lives.

Have you ever watched one of the many TV programmes that feature a family living in chaos? After an hour of clearing, renovation, and redecorating, their environment is completely changed. Have you noticed how the family isn't just living in chaos before the change? They are stressed out, anxious, frustrated, and sometimes even angry with each other. But once the home has undergone the transformation, they are more relaxed, less anxious, and happier! It's because our environment has a significant impact on our mood.

Take a look around your home. How does it feel? Is it cluttered? Clean? Peaceful? Do you enjoy the various spaces in your home, or is there a specific room or area you avoid? Making your home environment more enjoyable can take time and money, but it is more than worth it.

I owned a flat where the bathroom was dated when I bought it. I lived with that bathroom for five years before deciding to modernise it. Of course, once I did, I wondered why I hadn't done it sooner. It changed the entire energy of the flat I lived in. It also made me realise how I put up with something much longer than needed.

Sometimes the environmental problem is a bit deeper. It's not just about the home you're in. It's about the location of your home. Maybe it once suited you to live there because it met the needs of your life at that time. Perhaps it was close to your children's school, but they've grown up and moved out. We all evolve, and our needs change, or we realise they were never fully met in the first place. And locations can start to lose their charm. Living in an area you no longer love can affect your moods and the energy you bring to the rest of your life.

Is your environment affecting your life? Do you want to be closer to nature? Do you want more space? These are the questions to consider when creating the life you love.

I can hear the cries of 'But I can't take my children out of school!', 'How will I get to work?', or 'I don't think I can leave my extended family.' I understand all of this, and again, it's something only you can consider when looking at this area of your life. Also, remember that in the big scheme of your life, the environment may not be as important as you thought because other areas have a higher priority.

Changing location is a big decision and not for everyone, but if it brings you closer to the life you want, is it something you can push to the side and think about in a few years?

1. How did you come to live in your current location?

2. What do you like about your location?

3. What don't you like about your location?

4. If you could move anywhere else, where would that be?

5. What attracts you to living in your dream location?

6. If it is not possible right now to change location, what can you do to make your current location feel more like your dream location? For example, could you make

light home renovations to bring that dream location/environment closer? Could you make efforts to explore your current area more?

FINANCES & MONEY

I address money and money stories in Chapter 8, so I won't take too much time here. Money is always one of the top things that stop people from changing their lives. It is cited by people not choosing to take courses to further their education or change their careers, or in not being able to leave a job that no longer excites us. It is noted as the block to living where we would like to.

Working on your money story and challenging yourself in new ways of using your money can bring untold benefits to your life. It's about living from a place of abundance rather than scarcity. If money is an area you want to improve (and let's face it, who doesn't?), take your time with Chapter

8. I encourage you to look at the exercises in that chapter honestly to get the most out of them.

HEALTH

How is your health? Okay? Satisfactory? Without our health, we are nothing. Being and feeling healthy helps us to live the lives we want. In my research on people who have the lives they love, looking after their health is one of their top priorities. For them, giving their mind and bodies the exercise and nutrition they need helps to put them ahead in their lives.

And yes, I'm talking green juices, natural, unprocessed food, and little to no alcohol. When I mention this to clients or friends and family, I can see the look of 'Oh my God, how boring!' on their faces. Yet these very people complain about their lives or are looking for ways to change them but take no action.

I'm not saying drinking green juice daily will miraculously change your life, but it won't hurt you in the long run. Like many people, I went through a particularly sluggish patch for most of 2020 due to the pandemic. However, this carried on into 2021. I couldn't understand why I didn't have the energy I had the previous year, why I wasn't motivated to work on myself or my coaching business, or was feeling the way I was.

I had to do some tough reflection. I felt most energetic when I ate a vegan diet, exercised regularly, practised yoga and meditation, and drank less alcohol than I ever had. Then, I reverted to my pre-energetic self when the pandemic took hold in the UK. I ate a lot of food that comforted me — think spaghetti bolognese, lasagne, and carbs! I became scarily addicted to Jaffa Cakes (something I haven't touched since), and because of lockdown rules, I didn't go out as much to get fresh air or go for a walk. It became easy to sit indoors, pretend I was helping local businesses and the community by eating takeaways, and hibernating.

But this lifestyle took a toll, manifesting in weight gain, lethargy, increased anxiety, and poor sleep patterns. Most importantly, I began to lack the motivation to continue creating the life I'd started to envision for myself. This downturn in my health put a serious dent in committing to myself and the dreams I'd put down on paper. I started to second guess myself (another symptom of not looking after myself).

Being single and living alone, I didn't have anyone notice how quickly things were going downhill. I'd like to think if I'd been around family or friends a bit more, someone would have pointed out that I wasn't really myself. I have slowly crawled out of that place because I know how important my health is for me to reach the higher version of myself. If I don't take care of my body and mind, they won't take care of me, and I'd be stuck in the same demotivated, lacklustre cycle.

There are different ways to be and stay healthy, but you have to do what works for you. Not all of us want to spend time in a gym, and not all want to be runners. Most exercise regimes fail because we do activities that we don't enjoy. Once you find something that captures you, you are more likely to stick to it — and that's in all areas of life, not just health and fitness. If you like dancing, go dancing! If you like hiking, go hiking! Make moving your body something you enjoy doing because you want to keep active, not because someone is telling you that you need to in order to live a fulfilling life.

I've been that gym person, and I did it because it was suggested to me. I loved running, but Achilles inflammation has put an end to that. I had to find other ways to move my body. I've since returned to the gym, but my reason for going has changed. Before, it was about fitting in with others. Now it's about moving my body. Moving your body is as much about moving the energy inside you around your body as it is about keeping you mobile. If you sit still for long enough, your energy will also sit still. It won't go anywhere or be used for anything positive in your life. How can you create something you love by sitting still?

Look at what you're feeding your body. Look at how you are keeping your body moving. Is this how you want to continue? Do you want more energy and vitality? It's time to look at how to obtain that.

What changes could you make to improve your health and lifestyle? Record your answer below.

ROMANCE & RELATIONSHIPS

Caveat: This part of life may not be for everyone. Some people have no interest in romantic relationships or are taking a hiatus for one reason or another. If romance and relationships don't apply to you right now, skip to the next section. But if you're in a relationship or looking for a partner, examine what's going well and what can be improved.

When thinking about romance, many people believe it is only present in the first part of their relationship. This is commonly acknowledged when we say, 'The honeymoon period is over!' After that, we start to accept there may not be as much romance as there was in the beginning. But who said that romance was a limited-time offer in a relationship? If you consider romance important, don't you deserve to have the level of romance you want? Or do you feel the relationship has changed somewhat? Perhaps you're not getting the same feedback or intention from your partner that you did before.

Relationships tend to slip to the bottom of the list when life is busy. But intimate relationships need to be worked on just as much. If you don't nurture them, they won't grow along with all the other areas you work on. And sometimes, when you start to look at your relationship, it may mean having to make some tough decisions. Sometimes the relationship is not nurturing or meeting your needs, and you must decide whether it is worth staying.

Creating a life we love isn't always easy, and we must be completely honest about what we want and where we're willing to compromise. Relationships and a supportive, positive relationship are a priority for some of us. Working out what you want (and whether you're receiving it) can help you determine how balanced this area of your life is.

I've seen how staying in a relationship that isn't working affects nearly every other area of your life. I've watched friends remain in relationships because they were too scared to work on their self-esteem and find a much happier state of living. I've observed people lose their health, mental and physical, jumping through hoops to make a relationship work. There's nothing wrong with fighting for something you believe in. Still, in talking to some of these friends, none of them regretted leaving their relationships. They just wish they had done it sooner.

I've included one exercise for those of you who are in a relationship and another for those who are looking for one. You could do both if you're in a relationship but are looking for something different!

Already in a Relationship

    1. Think about the relationship you have. How long have you been together?

2. What areas of your relationship are you happy with?

3. What areas of your relationship would you like to improve?

4. What do you currently do to create the kind of relationship you want?

Looking for a Relationship

When we look for a relationship, we're looking for someone who meets our standards. Have you ever made a list of what you want in your perfect partner? Are the things you want surface-level desires, such as what a partner looks like? Or, do you desire attributes in your partner a bit deeper than looks alone? For example, what are their values? Do they want children? Do they support and align with your life views?

We often don't jump in and ask a potential partner certain things at the beginning of a relationship. Sometimes it can be much later that we start to talk about those things that are really important to us. Unfortunately, by that time, we may be too scared to leave the relationship, so we start to compromise.

You should be very clear about what you are willing to compromise before looking for a partner, or you could find yourself compromising on something or someone who doesn't meet what you want.

For this exercise (it can be a list or a description), I encourage you to seriously think about what you want in a partner. And yes, you can list all the superficial things as well! More importantly, get very clear about the things you definitely want and would not compromise on. It doesn't matter how good-looking or how good a cook a potential partner is. If they don't want to have children and children are important to you, it won't work.

Describe your perfect partner:

FAMILY & FRIENDS

As I've described earlier in this book, with my South Asian heritage, I was raised in a culture and tradition that valued family above all else. I'm talking about my immediate family plus my very large extended family. On more occasions than I care to remember, I was expected to attend extended family events because it was important to show up and represent the immediate family. There was always some family obligation that would override my wanting to do my own thing.

I also knew I was relatively lucky. Some South Asian families had many more events to attend than mine, and their parents were stricter than mine. But I still felt resentful because it seemed that life was just about being with family and doing what other people told me to do. There weren't many opportunities to explore what I wanted.

But that's not how life is. Once I got to a certain age, I could see other family members moving on with their lives and doing what they wanted, so where did the sudden obligation go? I always felt I had to be and do what others wanted.

It may sound like I dislike my family. Believe me, I don't! I love spending time with them, but I also know that if I spent all of my spare time with them, I wouldn't evolve and grow as my own person.

There's a saying that you are the sum of the five people you spend the most time with. Think about who those five people are in your life. Do you go along with things so that you fit in or don't upset anyone? If so, you might never (or rarely) think about what that means for you because you're too busy pleasing everyone else.

It can be an icky feeling to contemplate talking to others about this. I totally get that because family and friends are our people. And when we start to grow, we can feel it challenging to pull away from our loved ones. We don't want to leave them behind, and we can feel as if they won't love us anymore or won't agree with where we are moving in our lives.

Those feelings keep us in lives we don't always enjoy or no longer feel comfortable in. We keep ourselves small to appease others because we still think we must live by other people's rules. This doesn't mean you cut everyone out of your life and move miles away — unless that's truly something you do want to do. This is where you decide who gets access to you and for how long. This is where you determine how balanced your life needs to be, how much you want to see certain people and be involved in their lives, and how you want to be involved. You don't have to spend every waking moment with your loved ones to show you care and love them.

When you start setting boundaries and growing, be prepared that not everyone will agree with what you're doing. That's natural. When people — *especially* those closest to you — see you growing and shifting, they can feel threatened that their existence is not what *they* want, but they lack the courage to change it. So, be prepared for the negativity. It's up to you, though, whether you will be strong and stick to what you want or whether you allow yourself to be held back. Like everything in life, this isn't a one-time dance. It's a back-and-forth tango where you slowly inch further each time towards the life you want.

1. How many times per week or month do you see family or friends?

2. How many times per week do you spend with just yourself, your partner, and your children, without extended family?

3. How do you spend your time with your family or friends?

4. What activities would you like to participate in with your family or friends? Don't think about whether they would like them or not; this is about what you would like to do.

FUN & RECREATION

Wouldn't it be great if we could play all the time like we did when we were younger? Wouldn't it be wonderful if we didn't have to do the grown-up things like go to work or do household chores? If you create your life in the right way, there is no reason why you can't play more.

We stop being children usually because society has told us it's time to think about our future. We replace our hobbies with grown-up activities, like furthering our education, earning more professional qualifications, or networking with colleagues and clients.

There is a certain level of enjoyment to pursuing what interests us, but what happens when all of that isn't 'fun' anymore? The same thing occurs when any area of our life is out of alignment: We build up resentment, anger, and frustration, leaving us drained. At this point, many of us revisit the hobbies that inspired and kept us interested in life when we were younger. We rediscover or form friendships that aren't necessarily connected to our jobs. We create a boundary between our life and our work.

Another caveat: If you are one of the people who don't feel like their job is a 'job' but that it is, in fact, an extension of you or more like a hobby, then this section probably doesn't apply to you. If you are one of the lucky people with a job you don't want to take a holiday from, I am celebrating you. Why? Because I believe if any of us in life could have one thing, it would be a job we don't need a holiday from.

How do we get more fun and recreation in our life?

What is your definition of fun and recreation?

I recently had to think long and hard about these questions. A coaching programme exercise made me realise I wanted more fun and recreation in my life. That didn't mean I wanted to go out socialising all the time or to always participate in group activities.

Instead, I love learning new things. That is fun for me and has the added bonus of increasing my knowledge of whatever I'm learning about. I find going for walks in nature fun, but I don't find paddleboarding or training for running races fun. I prefer running just for enjoyment (I've learned that the hard way!). Fun and recreation are just that: *fun* and *recreation*. They're not something that has you regretting that you wasted hours on it. It's not something that you feel an achievement for but didn't actually enjoy doing. It's not something you do to keep other people happy or get validation from others.

I want to touch on something else: Joy is something we can all feel daily. But as we grow up, we're generally encouraged to be more serious about our lives — and we usually are not taught to keep the element of joy in our lives. It's almost as if we can have one or the other but not both. Or we get to only feel joy at certain times of the day — usually when we're not working! But joy is, as I said, something we can all feel every single day. It's something we have a right to do!

Fun and recreation are some of the most important acts of self-care. It consists of activities that fill up your energy reserves, that fill up that cup so that you can pour energy and love into other people.

1. Think about the last time you had fun doing something. What were you doing? How did it make you feel?

2. What activities would you like to make more time for in your life?

3. What activities do you know you *don't* like to do?

4. What does fun mean to you? There is no right or wrong answer here, and you don't have to answer how you *think* fun should be experienced. It's simply about what fun means to you.

PERSONAL GROWTH

Some people are content where they are in life. You and I both know people like this. They can include our family members, friends, colleagues, and people we socialise with. They don't seem interested in going outside their comfort zones because their life is already how they want it to be. (Or, it's not, and they lack the energy or motivation to change.) And that is perfectly okay for some people. There is no judgement here on that.

But there are also people, you and I, and people we know, who are not happy or content with the status quo. We want something more, and we *know* there is something more. We know that we are not the best version of ourselves. We want to experience growth and expansion of ourselves.

That growth can come in many forms. We may decide we want to learn a new skill to better our career — or desire a career change altogether. We may wish to explore our spirituality. We may like to travel or volunteer for charities we are passionate about. The ways we can grow are endless. Sometimes growth is as simple as wanting more confidence or changing our style — but it is growth all the same. What matters is that we expand from the person we are at that specific moment in time and that we affect some sort of change in ourselves, whether by ourselves or with the help of others.

There are times when our growth will be slower than at other times, purely because other priorities take precedence in our lives. But once we decide that personal development is important to us and we're aware that we want to have more of it, we will return to it again and again. It is ever-evolving, just like us.

As a coach and participant in many coaching programmes, I know how scary it is to spend a significant amount of money on something you can't physically see or touch. People can be reluctant to spend money on coaching because they can't visualise the results unless they've already had some coaching. A training course is different, as there is usually a certificate or qualification at the end. With coaching, the results could manifest as changes — *massive changes!* — in your life, relationships, or job. But until you are coached, you won't feel or see results.

Investing in yourself is one of the most important things you can do for personal development. It doesn't matter what the investment is for, but investing in yourself in this way puts skin in the game and keeps you showing up for yourself and your growth.

Now that you have some idea about the different areas of your life and what challenges you can face, I want you to use the answers from the exercise/s in the previous chapter.

1. What are the top three areas of your life you would like to work on?

2. Put these top three areas into priority order.

3. Write down the biggest change you'd like to see in each area. You don't have to think about solutions at this stage. Just identify what changes you want to see.

FINAL THOUGHT

I hope you're starting to see where you can make impactful changes in your life, bringing you closer to the life you want to live. I also understand if you are feeling overwhelmed or anxious about how to start making these changes. You'll learn in the next chapter how to manage your financial health and aptitude to more easily achieve your goals.

CHAPTER EIGHT:

MONEY MAKES THE WORLD GO ROUND

Too many people spend money they earned...to buy things they don't want... to impress people that they don't like.

— Will Rogers

I F WE'RE GOING to talk about building a life we love, then we have to talk about money. Like many of us, my clients worry about money — specifically, not having enough of it. We'd all like more money, right? This would allow us to live without restriction and afford everything we need and want. And when it comes to investing in yourself with courses, coaching, or further education, they all come at a cost. More money in the bank means more funds to devote to self-improvement.

Has there ever been something that you wanted to do that, had you done it, would have brought you much more happiness and possibly a better financial outlook for your life? Did you go ahead and invest in that for yourself? If you didn't, I don't want you to give me the reasons why not right now. We'll come on to that later in the 'Investing In Yourself' section of this chapter.

On top of being afraid to spend money on personal growth and development, most people live outside their means on a daily basis. Many earn a set income by working for other people and companies, whilst others work for themselves. Either way, the cost of services and goods we consume keeps rising, and it can be easy to have little to no money left in our bank accounts at the end of the month if we're not careful. This can cause a lot of stress.

I'm going to ask a question here, and as always, I want you to be honest with yourself: How regularly, if at all, do you look at your bank account? Is it never? Is it once a day, once a month, or once a year?

Would it surprise you that, according to the UK's Money & Pensions Service, more than 65% of people check their bank accounts weekly? That's more people than I had imagined. Some people check their accounts less often, some check them more often, and none of the answers is wrong.

What *is* important is that you are checking your finances regularly to see where your money is going and where you may need or want to make adjustments.

I've known people who have been too afraid to look at their bank accounts. It's because their account was in overdraft a lot of the time, which depressed them. But instead of acting to improve their situation, they preferred to remain in the dark. This only increased their stress level and didn't help the depression or anxiety they felt either. I know this because I used to be one of these people.

Becoming friends with your bank account and finances is the first step to financial success so that you can build that life you dream about. In this chapter, I want to take you through a straightforward understanding of finances. It may seem like I'm trying to teach you something you already know, but you would be surprised at how many people know this but don't apply the principles. Let's find out if you're one of them.

We'll look at the essential tasks of budgeting, handling credit and debt, and saving. Then we'll examine emotional issues that impact our relationship with money, including:

- How we use money to compete with others

- The stories we have around money

- How we perceive our worth

- How we address money in our relationships.

BUDGETING

Income vs. Expenditure

It may seem simple, but your expenditure MUST be less than your income if you want to live a financially responsible life. If your expenses are consistently above your income levels, you will find it challenging to meet your most basic needs, much less build up your savings or purchase luxury items. You must get comfortable with the figures and acknowledge where work is needed if you desire to become financially stable.

I've seen many people live a lifestyle they can't afford or sustain, and they end up creating more stress and challenges in their lives. 'Living in the present moment' is a phrase I've heard people use to justify spending habits. But this isn't what this phrase actually means! It doesn't mean spending all your money right now and not thinking about the future. The longer you continue this way, the more you won't actually be living. Instead, you'll only be surviving and existing to pay off all the bills you didn't consider whilst you were living in the present moment.

The Essentials: Fixed and Variable Costs

When creating the life you want, first identify the essentials. These are the fixed-cost items or services you can't do without: utilities, mortgage or rent, groceries, car payment, etc.

Next, consider your monthly variable costs like clothing, dining out, and personal care. Don't forget your mobile phone or Internet service provider. Do you really need that latest phone model, or could you use what you have for another year or two? Could you get by with a slightly lower-priced Internet package instead?

Changing your personal preferences can make a more significant impact than you think, especially with groceries. Switching to supermarket brands can help save you money that can be used elsewhere. Most of the time, these items are the same, just in different packaging.

Let's now look at luxury items. I split them into two categories because some things need more thoughtful money management than others.

Small Luxuries

Small luxuries include items like presents for family or friends, that morning latte, or personal entertainment like going to the cinema or out for meals. I include streaming services under this banner as they are not essential and can be budgeted around. Think about your gym membership. I've known quite a few people with a gym membership who don't often use it after the motivation wears off. And if you keep forgetting to cancel, that's money you can't use elsewhere.

Big Luxuries

Big luxuries are big-ticket items like a new car, family holiday, or home renovation you'll need to save up for. Or, you may take out a loan to have that desired thing now but end up paying more because of interest rates. Is it worth sacrificing a few things for six months to be able to pay for something in full, knowing you're not paying an extra lump sum of interest on top?

With clients who want to work on their finances, I have them write down every item they purchase for one or two weeks (e.g., not those essentials automatically paid for each month). This exercise will either bring my client the knowledge to move forward or send them deeper into hiding. It can be a shock to see how much money you are spending and where you are spending it — but that is the exact type of shock some people need to improve their financial management skills.

Once you know exactly where your money is going, you can adjust your spending habits to set yourself up for success and invest in what you really want in life. To do this, you must look at your finances and acknowledge where you are and where you would like to be.

As you probably know, completing a budget review is not a one-time exercise. I suggest looking at your budget at least every six months to ensure you are on track with spending and savings to make adjustments where necessary. This may sound like a chore, but I have done this for over fifteen years, and it has helped me know what is costing me more than I am willing to pay. As a result, I've cut back on specific areas and saved money in others. And I haven't felt I'm missing out or making do. I have a vision for my future and the life I want to create for myself, so I'm happy to keep doing this exercise.

I want you to get comfortable with how much money you have flowing in and out each month:

1. On a piece of paper, create two columns, one titled INCOMING and one titled OUTGOING.

2. Next, look at your bank account and write down each item and its cost for the last month in one of the categories I explained earlier in the chapter (fixed and variable essentials, small and big luxuries). Be honest!

3. If there are items that you have paid for in cash in the last month, write those down, giving them a category too.

4. Add up each column of the piece of paper to see which categories your money is going to.

This exercise will give you a rough idea of your income and expenditure. If you want to make it more accurate, I would suggest doing this for at least two continuous months so that you get to capture those items that don't get paid for from your bank account and which are not recorded anywhere.

You can also complete this exercise in a computer programme like Google Sheets or Excel, which provide the added benefit of auto-calculations and the ability to track expenses and income at a more detailed level that can be repeatable each month.

Bottom line:

Get to know exactly where your money is going! Develop a monthly budget and your financial priorities. Take advantage of the many good budgeting apps, or meet with someone you think handles their money well to help you teach you what they know. Then, conduct a review of where your money is coming from and how and where you're spending it. See how this data aligns with your priorities and make the needed changes. Challenge yourself to stick to your monthly budget.

CREDIT AND DEBT

Most people have some type of credit or debt to their name, from mortgages to loans and credit cards. When I was younger, I was taught that having any debt obligation beyond a mortgage was bad. Instead of viewing this as the warning it was meant to be, I took on a lot of debt through various credit cards and loans. I've definitely learned the hard way that while credit can serve a useful purpose, taking ownership of the resulting debt can limit the other choices you make in life.

Over the course of my adult life, I have had and paid off over £100,000 in debt. This didn't include mortgages but was purely credit card and loan debt. To make things worse, most of this debt was money I had loaned to a friend. Having been through this experience, I believe that if you have debt that isn't working for you but is working against you, you will not be able to build a solid financial foundation from which to build your dream life.

Mortgages work for us because when you eventually sell your home, it will hopefully be worth more than what you originally paid, leaving you with a profit to invest in your next home. Credit card debt used to purchase holidays and luxury items does not work for you. Unless you pay off your card in full every month to establish and maintain good credit, you will pay more for those items than you would have if you had saved and bought them outright.

My advice is to pay off your debts and save as much as you possibly can at the same time. I know this is easier said than done! The first time I had a lot of debt, my bank closed my accounts and sent the outstanding balances to a debt collection agency. I can't begin to describe the stress I felt at the time. For a few years I was getting daily phone calls demanding money and asking when I would pay the money back, something that deepened the depression I was already in.

It was not a great situation to be in when I was essentially at a stage of life where society thought I should be moving out on my own. I paid off that debt very slowly — and I had to learn how to budget quickly!

I was lucky that I was still living at home, so after my essential outgoings and debts were paid each month, I was left with a mere £15 a month to play with. This debt was relatively small in the big scheme of my total debt. But after paying this off, I still hadn't learned my lesson and ended up down the same path again because of my need for validation, fitting in, and keeping up. My lack of self-worth and desire to be the hero led to me loaning money to a friend (to the tune of nearly £70,000). I received less than 10% of this money back and shouldered that debt myself.

There's no denying that people exist on debt because of the societal structure of our modern culture — and most do so because they feel they have to fit in and want to be perceived a certain way by other people. So, it's not a surprise that in May 2022, the UK's Money Charity reported that the average total debt per UK household is nearly £65,000.

If only we had been taught how to make money work for us from a young age! Like many other areas of life, we take on the conditioning of people around us. We save, or we don't save. We have little respect for money, or we respect it too much.

Look at the people around you. Do you think they are all living financially secure lives? We are not taught that if we don't have money, we won't be able to do the things that matter to us in life. Instead, we are taught that it's easy to purchase something in the short term that we either don't need or lose interest in pretty quickly. It's hard to deny that we live in a 'want it now' society and have forgotten how to wait — if we ever even knew.

Being in debt can force us into situations we can find difficult to get out of. I got to a stage where I knew I either had to get a second job or strive to get a better-paid job. I went for the latter, and as much gratitude I have for these jobs helping me to reach my financial goals, they have hurt my Soul because these jobs did not light me up. They weren't, in my mind, helping humanity or trying to improve the world. They were jobs that helped other people become more prosperous than they already were. And that realisation in itself helped me to move my life forward. I wanted to do work that excited me and made an impact, even if it was just in one person's life.

I spent many years paying off my six-figure debt, and until that debt was paid off, I could not apply for a mortgage to buy a house. I ended up on the property ladder quite late in my life when banks and lenders were not in a rush to lend me money. My debt definitely limited my progress in life. There were educational and professional courses I wanted to do that I couldn't afford because I was (rightly) focused on paying off my debts. And it was frustrating at times because I could see other people moving on with their lives. I knew that if I wanted to create a decent life for myself (and at this time, I wasn't even looking long-term), I had to get rid of my debt.

You have to get comfortable with your debt before thinking about how to tackle it. I want you to look at your different types of debt, however scary this may feel.

1. Write down below (or on a separate sheet of paper or spreadsheet) each type of debt you have and the amount for each.

2. If you want to go further, track down the percentage interest you are paying each month and how long the remaining term is. This will show you the total amount you are paying and the financial mountain you must climb to pay it off.

How does this listing of your debts make you feel? It's hard to talk about how to solve your debt without addressing the topic of SACRIFICE.

What comes up for you when you hear this word? It isn't something that some people are willing to do. When they think of sacrifice, they believe they are being denied something and have no power over that sacrifice. Instead of learning the discipline of sacrifice, they continued in their ways, hoping their money troubles would somehow sort themselves out.

Let me share an example. A friend of mine had a good job earning more than the UK national average salary. This friend had rent and bills, but they also liked partying. When out with work colleagues or friends, they were one of the most generous people you could meet. Because of this, their nights out were rarely below the £100 mark and happened several times a week. This all started to add up, so I tried to help this friend with a budget and look at what they were spending on essential and luxury items. There is a saying: You can take a horse to water, but you can't make it drink. This is precisely what happened with this friend. I presented all the tools and ideas to help them climb out of debt and start saving, just as I had managed to do for myself, but they could not let go of their nights out.

It's hard to see a way out of debt when you're in it, and not all of us have additional financial support to help erase that debt. I didn't; I was in a single-income home and was too embarrassed to ask my family for help. So, I made sacrifices. I didn't go out for meals or nights out as often as I had previously. I didn't go on holiday. I didn't make big purchases that I didn't need. Eventually, I got myself out of debt and into a place where I was able to save money and experience more financial peace — and that's why I try to help others do the same.

Bottom Line:

Having a handle on your money brings a certain level of freedom and fewer restrictions to living the life you want. Educate yourself on how to properly use credit to your advantage. Avoid discretionary debt (e.g., items other than a mortgage or car payment) as much as possible. This is a lesson in restraint that requires every ounce of 'adulting' in you, but trust me when I say that your future self *will* thank you!

SAVINGS

I've talked a lot about spending money and avoiding the debt trap, but what about saving? Speaking to family, friends, and work colleagues, I've heard how people find it challenging to save money because they have so many debts and bills to contend with. When they feel like this, they don't see the point of even trying to save because it seems like a task that is too difficult.

I felt the same way when I was paying off my mountain of debt. I didn't know how I would be able to save money. What was the point if I still had so much debt to pay? But I finally realised that if I didn't start saving, I would never be able to afford to buy a house, go on holiday, or adequately prepare for my future.

So I began to save money, even if it was just a few pounds a month. I put into a savings account whatever I could spare. I had a tin at home where I would put my loose change, and once it was full, I would take it to the bank and put it in my savings account. It wasn't hundreds of pounds, but it added up. I would get a spark of excitement when I put money away and watched my little nest egg grow. That encouraged me to keep saving — *and* to keep looking at where I was overspending or wasting money.

Many believe that we must save significant amounts of money each month, or it isn't worth it. If we can set aside more money a month, then great! But with rising living costs and salary levels not increasing, people find it challenging to meet their obligations, let alone find money to put away for a rainy day. But I stand by the act of saving whatever is possible because it will start to add up.

I mentioned before that I used to have a tin to put my loose change in, and then I would take it to the bank when it was full. Because we live in a society that is fast becoming cashless, I've found I no longer have much loose change. It is convenient to tap my debit card at the register or use my smartphone rather than pay with money. There are apps now that can round up transactions and transfer what would effectively be the loose change into a separate account. You may not physically be able to touch the money, but it has the same end result in helping you to save it.

Answer the following questions:

1. Do you save money each month (however little)?

2. If not, what stops you from doing this?

Now, consider what could be a comfortable amount of money you could put away or whether one of the many financial apps could help you save your loose change. If you take the first option, check back in three or six months and see how you are doing. If you've chosen the app, review it after a month and see how much money gets transferred from the transactions you are making.

Bottom Line:

It doesn't matter how little you save, but I would encourage you to start if you don't already do so. Put that money in an account without easy access. Make sure you don't touch it and let it grow, however slowly that may be — because, in time, it *will* make a difference. It may seem unachievable initially, and if it helps, give yourself a goal.

Establish a number you want to reach by a specific date. Or price up something that you want to buy and work towards saving for that. Again, the goal is to simply start.

We could explore other money management topics beyond budgeting, credit and debt, and saving, but I trust you to keep educating yourself on the money basics and beyond. I think it's more important to pivot to address the heart of most financial matters, and that's our emotional relationship to money — namely, how we use money to compete with others, the stories we have around money, how we perceive our worth, and how we address money in our relationships. Let's dive in.

KEEPING UP WITH THE JONESES

This phrase about not being outdone by one's neighbours was thrown about a fair bit in the 80's and early 90's. People had more disposable income and started to spend it on luxury items like gadgets for the home, cars, and holidays abroad. Up until then, there had still been a certain level of frugality in England. But this idea of 'Keeping up with the Joneses' was most likely (in my humble opinion!) the start of people going into debt to be seen as being at the same place in life as everyone else.

My parents grew up when things were not readily available on credit, so they saved up money before making big purchases. Perhaps your parents did the same. Many of us now have larger disposable incomes, credit is more readily available, and online shopping is the norm, making purchases more instant. This helps us make decisions much more quickly; sometimes, those decisions don't always benefit us.

My parents never followed what others were doing. It didn't matter if someone else's family was going on holiday in the UK or abroad; we didn't go on holiday because the money wasn't there for us. Yes, we had days out in the summer holidays, but we never went away. I always dreaded going back to school and telling the class what I had (or, more accurately, *hadn't*) done in our time off.

Additionally, it's no secret that social media can greatly impact our spending habits. Influencers obtain contracts to advertise products to their followers. It is easy to be persuaded by someone we admire to buy the same thing they have used and found to benefit them. It isn't any different from our family, friends, or work colleagues telling us about something they've bought or somewhere they've been. Our minds can tell us we need to do the same, even if it's not something we truly desire for ourselves. Before we know it, we're regretting that purchase and wish we had spent the money on something else or saved it instead.

It is a little different as I've grown older and see my nieces and nephews attending school. Thanks in part to social media (again, in my humble opinion), comparing or being compared to others has become second nature. If you are the one who is not doing what everyone else is doing, or you are the one who doesn't have what everyone else has, then it's easy to be seen as the outcast. Some parents now find it more difficult to say no to their children because they don't want them to be bullied. So, they may be more apt to give in to their children's desires, even if that means building up debt or having to sacrifice things for themselves.

I know mothers who will always put their children before themselves. They will do without social activities, clothes, and other things so their children will not go without. They will meet the short-term whims of their child so that they don't look bad in front of their peers and can go through life with ease.

I completely understand this, but what does it teach our children? That every demand you make will be met? That someone will always give you everything you want? That it's easy to fulfil every need you have?

These are the wrong messages we send out, especially if we are not talking to our children about the sacrifices it takes to meet those demands and needs. And it's not about making them feel guilty. It's about teaching children that money has value and that in our society, to get money, something else has to be sacrificed. This often means giving our time and skills in the form of our jobs.

If we don't teach our children this and prepare them to set out on their own, they'll be more prone to turn to credit cards and loans to continue funding the lifestyle they grew up with. And so the debt mounts, and they get caught in the same debt cycle — and that's something none of us wants!

In the Credit and Debt section earlier in this chapter, I had you write down your total amount of debts and what they are.

Now I want you to think about how much of your expenses are tied to pressure you may feel to keep up with others. It is crucial that you are honest with yourself here! Look at your list and ask yourself why these things matter to you. Do those items truly align with your personal goals for living the life you want to live? What could you give up? Write these things down below.

Bottom Line:

Trying to keep up with the Joneses is a losing battle. It only breeds discontent and keeps you locked in a never-ending 'grass is always greener' cycle. Take control of your financial situation and make sure your actions (including what you buy) match your life goals. Live within your means and find contentment with what you have and can comfortably afford. If you honour your financial goals and what truly brings you joy, you won't feel the need to keep up with anyone else.

MONEY STORIES

If we want to live a life of financial freedom, we not only have to become friends with our bank accounts and finances, but we also have to look at what stories we tell ourselves about money and its role in our life.

Our family of origin influences us from an early age in managing different aspects of our life, including how we think about and manage our money. On top of this, society has made money embarrassing to talk about. If you are well off and talk about what you are doing with your money, you can be seen as boastful. Or, it can be embarrassing to admit you are struggling if you don't feel well off. Employers don't like their employees talking about salaries because they don't want employees negotiating pay rises they may not be able to honour.

I remember my first 'proper' job. Fifteen of us started in a group internship with the same salary, except for one guy. He was on more than the rest of us because he had a degree but did precisely the same job. None of us had any prior industry knowledge, but his degree earned him higher pay simply because he had studied for a few more years.

Was I annoyed when I found out? Yes, because I worked on the same team and was always given more complex work than him. It's a hard fact of life that most well-paid jobs usually demand a certain level of education. Not that it is always necessary for the job, but it seems to be something that is still viewed as essential in specific roles. I don't have a degree, and I never went to university — and I allowed this 'money story' that I could never make a good salary because of my perceived lack of education hold me back for many years.

In time, I realised that when working for others, I needed to learn my worth and negotiate my own wage. This isn't always easy, especially if a job is advertised at a specific salary. But there is nothing to stop you from asking for extra when you go for an interview.

One of my clients' top money stories is that they don't feel worthy enough to be paid more than they currently earn. It is also a driving factor for leaving a job to go to another company that will pay them what they feel they are worth. And this is exacerbated by people wanting a different lifestyle or wanting to improve their lives. They look to their employer to provide the means for them to create the life they want. This is giving power away to someone else.

If you can relate to this, you need to know you can take control. It comes from learning how to use money to create money so that you can generate different income streams. Again, it's not something that is taught to many of us. And if our parents or those around us didn't look to other income sources, we would not be exposed to learning how to do those things for ourselves. Even simple budgeting was not taught when I went to school, and from listening to parents with children at school, it still isn't happening. No wonder we are a society struggling with debt.

 ACTIVATION

1. What did you learn about money from the people around you as you grew up?

2. How have these stories affected your view on money and impacted your life?

3. How would you like to change any money stories you are holding on to?

Bottom Line:

If we want to create a life we love, we have to take responsibility for the stories we tell ourselves about money — and then learn how to write a different ending, one that supports our worth, our dreams, and the life we want and deserve to live.

INVESTING IN YOURSELF

When I first started working, I knew nothing about investment in myself. My perception was that my employer would be the one investing in me by providing me with ongoing training and courses that would improve my career prospects. This wasn't always the case though, especially when the economy started to take a downturn in the mid-nineties and budgets were cut at work. I found myself being passed over for courses because my employer couldn't afford to send all staff on the courses that they wanted to do, even though this would also impact salary increases and bonuses when end-of-year reviews were conducted.

I soon learned that the only way for me to improve my skills and employability was to start investing in myself and what I could offer potential employers. My investments at the time went as far as office and computer skills. I thought that spending money on a creative writing course, a money management course or language course was frivolous and wouldn't help me get on in the world. How wrong was I! That money management course would most likely have saved me a lot of stress and struggling in figuring out things for myself. Investing in myself always felt that it was to help me get a better job, never about developing myself so that I could live a better life.

There are so many ways a person can invest in themselves. If you're wondering why it is so important to invest in yourself, know this: If we don't continue to learn, we don't continue to grow. And if you don't want to grow, that is perfectly okay. But if you want to grow, there is only one way of doing it. It is to expand into the next version of you. The version that has improved or found new skills. The version that understands family dynamics more deeply so that you can create a stable and loving home. The version who is learning to use your money to make money so that you can cut down your hours at your 9-to-5 job. The list is endless.

We can't do this all by ourselves; I have learned that. Walking that path on your own will only get you so far. There will come a point when you will need help from someone who has already walked that path. Whether that help comes in the form of a book, a training course, a mentor or a coach, to get the growth you desire, you must invest in yourself, and yes, I do mean financially. I can't emphasise enough that seeking out people who have already done what you want to do and getting help will fast-track you to where your Soul knows you want to be.

Many of us, especially women, have money blocks around spending money on ourselves. We are taught to stay frugal and save for the future. But what if getting to that future required you to invest in the now? To live the future you want, you would have to spend some of that hard-earned cash and invest in something that could benefit you in the longer term.

Think about where you are in your life right now. It may help to go back to the Wheel of Life for this.

1. What areas of your life would you invest in if money were no object?

2. What type of things would you invest in (e.g., a training course to increase job prospects, a more reliable car, etc.)?

Bottom Line:
Investing in yourself is not selfish. It is, in some ways, selfless. Because it will not only be you who benefits from the investment. It will be your loved ones, your family, your friends, your employer or your business. Your investment in yourself will impact the world around you. Who are you to deny the world the next version of you?

MONEY & RELATIONSHIPS

If you're in a committed relationship, do you talk to your partner about money? You would be surprised how many couples don't discuss finances or examine how they want to finance their dream life together.

I knew a couple with so much debt who lost everything because they didn't get the support or help they needed before the problem got out of hand. I also know couples who are constantly living month-to-month despite having more than enough money to finance their lifestyle, all because they've never talked about what they wanted to achieve financially in their relationship. And there are couples I've known with joint and individual accounts who speak about the future and how to finance it.

I'm sure you know stories of people only being in relationships because of their partner's wealth. Money in relationships can create power struggles. When one person earns or has more money than the other, it can be easy for them to feel like they have the upper hand in the relationship. And if you are the person who has less money, it can make you feel inferior or like you don't have as much say in the relationship. Letting money get in the way of how your relationship works is only going to end one way, so you both must be aware and in agreement on how your money works for you.

In my twenties, I had a friend living with a man who earned most of the money in their relationship. They decided to travel and eventually settled in New Zealand. However, whilst there, he could pick up work due to his skills, but she couldn't. This meant that he became the breadwinner, and she would ask him for money when their travel budget had run out.

I was shocked when I heard this. I couldn't imagine letting someone else decide how much money I was allowed in order to live my life. I'm sure it's been one of several factors in my wanting to be financially independent and always provide for myself, regardless of what anyone else may bring into my life.

I also took it as a hangover from the '50s and '60s when women were encouraged to stay at home and run the household based on an allowance from their husbands. Of course, women have become much more financially independent, and they now also go out to work and, in some cases, become the household's primary breadwinner. But this can also harm a relationship. Men can feel emasculated because they've been raised to provide for their family, and here they are, letting their wife or partner do that instead. Don't get me wrong, not all relationships are like this, but if your relationship shows hints of power struggles because of money, it needs to be addressed sooner rather than later.

For some, it's not an issue which partner earns more. Ideally, both partners would be working towards the same goals. I know couples at different levels of their careers but how they combine and make their money work for them makes all the difference in how they live their life.

If you are in a relationship, I'd like you to consider the following. As always, be honest with yourself!

1. Do you and your partner speak about your joint and individual finances? If not, why is this?

2. How do you and your partner prepare financially for unplanned circumstances, such as losing a job or long-term health issues?

3. How would you like you and your partner to handle your finances going forward? Are you working towards the same financial goals?

Bottom Line:

There are many ways in which couples decide to manage their finances. No one way is right or wrong, as long as the finances *are* managed and support you in creating the life you envision. If it's not working, just know it can be changed, though it may take some tough conversations for that to happen.

FINAL THOUGHT

One of the very best things you can do for yourself in life is to become financially literate. And there is no lack of resources. Read books on the subject, check out your banking institution's educational services, or consider meeting with a financial planner or accountant.

Money is a form of energy that we exchange for the things we want and need in our lives. But many of us believe that money gives us worth and makes us look good to others, including our partners.

To create and live the life we want, we have to have the means to do it — no two ways about it. And that means acknowledging, becoming friends with, and taking control of your money. It means knowing what you want to do with your money and what you want your money to do for you. It means knowing when to sacrifice and cut back to ultimately have more.

Looking Ahead

We've covered a lot of ground in Parts 1 and 2, addressing Soul issues, life balance, and money. You've worked through almost seventy prompts, and digging into these concepts will provide a steady foundation for moving through the issues we address in Part 3, *The Challenges*.

In Chapter 9, *15 Common Blocks to Your Dream Life*, we delve even deeper into self-exploration, so plan on spending as much time as you need to work through the fifty-plus prompts. We'll conclude Part 3 with a short chapter on mental health before moving on to discovering our way forward in Part 4.

You're doing great work here. Keep it up!

PART THREE

203

CHAPTER NINE:

15 COMMON BLOCKS TO YOUR DREAM LIFE

Your present circumstances don't determine where you can go; they merely determine where you start.

– Nido Qubein

I WAS DEEP into my self-development journey before I realised the many ways I was blocking myself from having the life I wanted. As soon as I started to examine these blocks impacting my mindset and beliefs, my life started to change.

In this chapter, we'll review 15 common blocks many of us impose on ourselves that slow down our self-development journey. Why so many? Let's just say there seems to be no end to our creative abilities to self-sabotage!

- People pleasing
- Not saying yes to you
- The Sacred No
- Lack of time
- Impatience
- Lack of self-belief
- Lack of boundary setting
- Not exercising your power of choice
- Not taking back your power
- Fear of getting what you want
- Waiting for 'perfect' conditions
- Comparison and jealousy
- Age
- Procrastination
- The fear of letting go

Whether you relate to all or some of these, know it is never too late to remove these blocks from your life. I provide exercises for each block we discuss to help you move past them.

If you're willing to do the work, a clearer path to living the life you genuinely want awaits you.

PEOPLE PLEASING

I've been a people pleaser for most of my life, largely because my mother, aunts, and their mothers were people pleasers. My culture drives home that as a woman, I — like my mother and aunts — was expected to put other people before myself. It meant ensuring everyone else was attended to before I cared for myself. My needs didn't matter as much as others' desires, including those who didn't like me. It didn't matter if those people were nice to me; I was taught to treat everyone how I wanted to be treated.

At home, I was expected to forego any personal activities if they clashed with a family event. There was an expectation that family came before everything else because they would always be there for you. This family-first mentality is impressed on many of us, not just in my culture. It fosters a community spirit but can cause us to stop looking out for ourselves. And I had learned all of this before I'd even joined the workforce, where people pleasing is elevated to an entirely different level!

As I got older and went to work in sometimes toxic environments, I suppressed my voice of truth. As a people pleaser, I thrived on validation from my managers and peers. To achieve this, I did things I didn't want to or weren't in alignment with my Soul — which only blocked me from progressing in my life. Even though I spent much of my life seeking validation outside of myself, I rarely felt satisfied or happy.

That's the thing about pleasing others. It won't matter who you please and what you do to please them. You'll end up feeling resentful, unsatisfied, and unhappy. Yes, the feeling that you've done something nice for someone else may last a little while and give you a faint glow. But when that glow is gone, and you remember you had to cancel a night out with friends or sacrifice time with family to meet another deadline, those feelings of resentment and anger will start to bubble up again.

In May 2018, I went on a solo weekend trip to Budapest, where I serendipitously picked up and read *The Life-Changing Magic of Not Giving a F**k* by Sarah Knight — and it was transformative for me. I had spent much of my life putting others before myself. When I finished reading, I knew I had to take back my time and my life. Although the book focused on not wasting time on things we don't want to do, it opened my eyes to much more.

That book also helped me realise that whilst I was doing what everyone expected of me, no one else appeared to do the same. Most people I knew seemed to show up to events only when they felt like it or help out at work only when it benefited them. They weren't living by the same standards I thought I had to live by. Why was I allowing these expectations to drive my life when others seemed to be able to shrug them off?

At that time, I didn't know about my Sacred No (discussed later in this chapter). That book pulled it out of me. It wasn't easy to start saying no to things I never wanted to do in the first place. It didn't please other people, either.

As I've mentioned earlier in this book, I would spend many lunchtimes in pubs, with co-workers, drinking excessively, mainly in an effort to fit in. This people-pleasing behaviour, in turn, blocked me from progressing in my life. My dreams of being a clothes designer, a writer, or a nutritionist were pretty hard to fulfil with a near constant hangover. Thankfully, as I also wrote about, a new job came along that allowed me to leave the toxic work environment I was in, leading to less alcohol consumption. For once, I had a sense of clarity I hadn't had in years.

I also read Knight's *You Do You: How to Be Who You Are and Use What You've Got to Get What You Want*. Among other things, it addresses how we place expectations on others based on our conditioning and upbringing. Some of us might expect our siblings to be there for us at all stages of our lives, regardless of where they are or what they're doing. Or, we want our friends to pick up every time we call. Many of us expect our jobs to fulfil our career dreams.

When none of these outcomes happen, we become disappointed, frustrated, angry even. But we keep feeling obligated to be all of these things to others. We do this because we want others to like us. But Knight's book taught me how to put myself first.

Here's a secret: When other people do not meet the expectations we put on them, it's usually because they are putting themselves first. It's not because they don't like us or care about us. It's because they are putting themselves, their families, and their dreams and desires first — something we have failed to do. And isn't that really how it should be when creating the life you want? Are you building a life you want for yourself or a life that someone else wants for you?

Take a look back at your life and reflect on the following questions:

1. In what situations have you found yourself pleasing others rather than yourself?

2. Where have you expected others to please you rather than please themselves?

3. What things have you not done because you have put others before yourself?

4. What things would you like to pursue if it meant no one would feel upset if you put yourself first?

NOT SAYING YES TO YOU

When was the last time you said yes to you? And I mean *really* said yes, where you put yourself first before taking care of everyone and everything else in your life. Saying yes to yourself goes hand in hand with Your Sacred No (see the next section) — because Yes and No are two sides of the same coin.

Saying yes to ourselves is not something that usually comes naturally. Many of us have been raised to believe our needs and desires aren't as important as those of others. We've learned to put ourselves at the bottom of the list.

Here's the thing: When you say yes to something, you are saying no to something else — and that is usually you.

Much of this comes down to how we feel we'll be perceived if we put ourselves first. Has anyone ever called you selfish because you dared to put yourself before them? I've heard it a few times in my life. I've had friends say I'm selfish because I chose time alone rather than another afternoon of drinking with them.

Or perhaps you have people in your life who won't directly accuse you of being selfish but rather act in a passive-aggressive manner that has you in no doubt that they disagree with your decision. They may stomp off, give you the silent treatment, or distance themselves — all because you deign to choose yourself for a change!

This type of behaviour can manifest in all areas of our life: with our partners, families, workplaces, and social circles. Sometimes we say yes to events and obligations to keep the peace, which only emphasises to ourselves and others that we aren't the most important player in our own lives. Everyone gets the memo that they're more important and how we end up feeling doesn't matter. Is that really the message you want to send?

And if you're a people-pleaser, then it's also natural that you don't want to disappoint people by saying no to them. Remember this: That person may not know that when you say yes, you may be berating yourself for that decision. You are the sole audience member hearing this internal monologue. So, there you may be at an event you'd rather not attend, with heightened anxiety — and while some people may pick up that you seem 'off,' they likely won't have an accurate clue about what's happening inside you.

It would've been easier to say no in the first place, right? But it takes time to get to a point where we can do that because of our upbringing and conditioning as we grow up.

I mentioned before that I was raised in a Sikh household where family obligations came above anything else. If a relative came to visit, my mum would call me to come downstairs and be sociable, even if it was only my uncle or cousins who lived close by. I'd dutifully sit there for what felt like hours, smiling and nodding along when in reality, all I was thinking about was the deadline I had to meet for a college assignment. There was never any question of saying no until I moved out of the family home.

Once I did leave home, it became easier to say yes to myself and no to family demands. Yes, I told a few white lies here and there, but I also became more confident in saying I didn't want to go. The more I chose myself over others, it became easier to say no to others. And now, if I don't want to do something or am not feeling up to it, I won't. But it took a lot of practice to get there, and it didn't happen overnight.

Ask yourself: Do you want to keep living a life where other people have more say in how you do things and what you do? Or do you want to create a life where you put yourself first and have a full cup to pour from? Because that is the other side of this. When you say yes to yourself more often and pursue more of your dreams, it becomes easier to say yes to other people and opportunities.

You feel less resentful and angry that you don't have time for yourself because you've already made that time for yourself. You've already ensured you've taken care of your needs first. There isn't any question about helping others out or being there for someone else because you have already made sure that you've taken care of yourself. It may sound simple, but changing how we do things takes time. And it may raise eyebrows with others, but this isn't about them. This is about *you* and *your* life.

I'll ask the question again: Do you want to keep living a life where other people have more say in how you do things and what you do? Or do you want to create a life where you put yourself first and have a full cup to pour from?

I know which one I would, and have, chosen. When you say yes to yourself and take action on the things you want, it can inspire others to change their lives. And by saying yes to yourself, you are signalling to the Universe that you want more of the good stuff. Yes, the Universe gets involved in everything!

I want you to have a life you truly enjoy and have created for yourself. I don't want you to be stuck in a life where you are going along with what other people want for you. I want you to learn to say yes to *you*!

Think about where you say yes in your life. Think about whether this is a natural reaction or if you take a breath before you say yes. Over the next week, I want you to notice when someone asks you for a favour, asks you to help them out, or to meet up. Are you saying yes instinctively, or are you waiting before you say yes?

How do your observations make you feel? Are you happy with how you reacted, or is this something you would like to work on? If you want to work on this, try this: Whenever you are asked for something, stop for a moment. Use one of the following prompts to give yourself more time before you commit to something:

1. Can I get back to you on that?

2. Let me check my diary.

3. I'll let you know.

It can take a bit of practice, but I promise it will be worth it!

Saying Yes To You When Others Are Involved

Creating your own life is the ultimate act of loving yourself: It's a big YES to yourself and what you want in life. It's about putting yourself first before you help others so you can help others more readily.

But what happens when others are involved? If you have a partner, children, or other dependents, saying yes to you can feel overwhelming and even impossible. You may be ready to change your life, but your partner is comfortable and doesn't see the need for change. Maybe your children are settled in their routines and schools, even though they might benefit from a happier parent who is more in tune with what they want from life. (Plus, it would provide an excellent example of how to create their *own* lives!)

What then?

In this situation, you need to share how what you desire will positively impact your loved ones. Start by making small changes. Don't go for the big dream straight away. When your loved ones see how beneficial this is for you (and them), it'll help ease their fears that you will leave them all behind. And this is what I've found to be the biggest challenge when people start saying yes more to themselves: It's others' fears that they'll be left behind that stop us from pursuing what we want. And that fear can cause us to hold off on making any changes.

No Way Back

There is one problem, though. Once you know you want to change your life, there is no turning back. One of my mentors, Preston Smiles, often says, 'You will have to lose your old life to create your new one.' Once you know you are on the path of change, how can you possibly return to what was there before?

How can you know that you really don't like your job but then decide that retraining, looking for a new employer, or pursuing that promotion feels too daunting? How can you know that your health is not as great as you want it to be but continue to eat the same things every day and not improve your health because it feels difficult?

Remember, you don't have to change everything at the same time! I know it sometimes feels like our entire life needs an overhaul. But you don't have to change everything all at once. It's better if you don't! Small changes can bring big impacts. And often, your changes will filter into other areas of your life. For example, switching jobs can provide you with more energy and enthusiasm, financial freedom, or extra time to pursue your interests.

There may be times you want to give up. I'm not going to lie; there were times when I wondered why I was so intent on changing things that were ticking along nicely. And those times felt difficult because I wasn't seeking the support I needed to lovingly push me ahead.

While it can be easier to make decisions when you don't have anyone else to answer to or consider, it can be challenging to take the leap without any support from anyone else.

I've been fortunate to find people who have changed their lives and have seen how much I want to make similar changes. I would encourage you to do the same. Find that community that can support you from a place of impartiality. If you admire how a friend made positive changes in their life, ask them how they did it, including the challenges they faced. They'll probably become your biggest cheerleader. People who have made significant life changes are usually happy to help others do the same by giving advice, the occasional loving push, and any other support you need.

Also, don't forget this isn't a one-time process. Making changes can happen many times in your life. There is so much more to life than the big goals of settling down with a good job, a beautiful home, a nice car, an amazing partner, and adorable children. Life is not done when you check any or all of these items off the to-do list. In fact, for many of us, this is where it all starts. We don't feel satisfied, and we want something more.

That's the reason you chose this book. You want something more. So, even when you have created what you feel is a good life, don't be disheartened if you have the urge to change things up in a few years. This is usually a sign that your life needs a little tweak — but you must have the courage to listen and discern how to say yes to what's best for you.

1. How often do you say yes to events and requests from others and wish you hadn't?

2. How often in your life would you say that you put your own dreams and wants aside to help someone else with theirs?

3. What things do you wish you had the courage to say yes to?

4. What would you want to do if there were no restrictions in your life? There are no limitations here!

5. Why haven't you done what you've identified above?

THE SACRED NO

The other side of saying yes to yourself is learning to utilise the Sacred No. Why is it called the Sacred No? I think it's because many of us don't exercise this word in our lives. And if we do, it's not very often. We are so used to saying yes to others that no gets erased from our vocabulary. So, when we do say no to something or someone, it can feel sacred — transformative and divine.

I've recently seen more people expressing their Sacred No. Maybe the global pandemic has something to do with it. Many things have shifted for people in response to what has been happening in the world. People started to realise what mattered or was no longer a priority for their happiness. They had the opportunity to change how they responded to requests on their time and resources. They had the chance to put themselves first because they had no choice but to do so.

I remember working from home during the pandemic, living alone in my flat. For what felt like the first time in my life, I didn't have to consider anyone in what I was doing. If I wanted to read all day, no other social events were vying for my attention. If I wanted to go for a walk, I didn't have to fit it around other events or demands that typically would have taken up my time. This provided freedom I and many others haven't felt in a long time.

Employing our Sacred No matters because it helps us live a life of our own making. Doing so doesn't make you selfish. It's just that your priorities are different from someone else's. And you don't have to justify your no. That is something we are also very good at. As soon as we say no, we reel off an explanation for why we are saying no. That isn't needed. We don't have to tell people why we don't want to accept an offer or don't want to do something we are asked to do. It's not their business.

Saying no is crucial if we want to protect ourselves emotionally and physically. Saying yes to most things in your life can leave you physically and emotionally drained, especially if these are things you don't enjoy or are feeling goaded into. Saying no to others means you have said yes to yourself. And when you are creating a life you love, that is something to be honoured.

How you say no also matters. I've said no before, a bit half-heartedly, which opened the door for the other person to start encouraging me to change my answer. And on about 95% of occasions, I usually did. Did I regret giving in? Mostly, yes. And mainly because it took time away from the things important to me.

Saying no can have a massive impact on your life if you let it. It takes courage to keep expressing your Sacred No, so I've created an exercise to help you strengthen that 'no' muscle.

1. For the next week, I want you to say no to two or more requests each day.

2. Write down what or to whom you said no and how you felt afterwards.

3. Notice where you are justifying your no, or explaining why you are saying no. And notice who you find it easy to say no to or where you find it more difficult to exercise your no.

LACK OF TIME

Lack of time is one of the most common challenges my clients face. They are so busy doing it all and caring for everyone else that they barely have time for themselves. And this can become a barrier to making changes in their lives.

Some people will tell you there is no such thing as time; it is only a construct. We use time to structure our days and activities, but what did people do before the invention of sundials and clocks? They just went about their business, doing tasks when they needed to.

We don't seem to have such 'time luxury' anymore. Instead, we are constrained by time. We have to be at certain places at certain times, and we must spend specific hours at work or school. We do this so we can collapse at the end of the day, wondering where that time went!

Given the often frantic pace of our modern world, it's natural that many of us want freedom from common time restraints. If we're being honest, we'd admit that we want to do the things we want — and when we want to do them. We'd concede that we don't want someone else telling us where and how long we should be somewhere.

Being constrained to such rigid time commitments was one of the main reasons I wanted to leave my corporate job. For years, I woke up with the explicit purpose of being at my desk by a specific time each day. And I would spend at least eight hours there before I was 'allowed' to go back home. When I was based in London but working for an Australian company and saw that a 9-to-5 job didn't have to actually be 9am to 5pm, it got me thinking about how to create a life where I had some control over the days and hours I worked.

How would you feel if you had a certain amount of work to do, but it didn't matter if it took you a few hours or days to do it? Sounds great, doesn't it? And granted, this doesn't work for every type of job, but we are seeing more companies move to a more flexible work model.

This option, of course, has become more acceptable due to work-from-home requirements during the pandemic. Companies have seen the traditional 9-to-5 work day give way to a more flexible work schedule that many agree has resulted in greater productivity. Control over your work schedule can free up time during the day to take care of errands or plan self-care like a massage. Again, this flexibility doesn't work for every kind of job. Still, it's a conversation worth having with your employer if your need for a better work-life balance is causing you to rethink the viability of your current work arrangement.

For some, the time management issue extends beyond the daily schedule to a broader feeling that they are running out of time to make significant changes or improvements in their lives.

I've seen this phenomenon bear out with work colleagues who've spent twenty-plus years in a particular industry and don't feel the freedom to pivot to something else. They rationalise that they'd have to start on the bottom rung of the career ladder again, would waste the experience they've gained, or would have to learn from younger colleagues.

These internalised fears keep a person stuck. Instead of trying new things, it is comforting and more suitable to stay where they are, even if it means they spend the next decade complaining about their job! As the saying goes, 'The devil you know is better than the devil you don't!'

I've also seen people close to me struggle more personally with the idea of time running out. They've gotten into a routine that feels too difficult to change up, and it can seem easier to keep going to the same places on holiday or to the same restaurant for the same favourite dish. They feel it's too late to change what they like to do.

Can you relate? Please know this: It's *never* too late. If you knew you had another forty (or even four!) years on this planet, would you carry on doing what you are doing? If you're craving something more out of life, do you really want to spend your future, however long that may be, doing precisely the same thing as you're doing now?

Now is the time to learn new things, visit new places, and try new activities. These all keep the brain active and your Soul excited. It doesn't matter how young or old you are, and it doesn't matter where you are in your life. Yes, it can feel uncomfortable when you try something new, and venturing beyond your comfort zone usually brings necessary discomfort. This feeling doesn't last forever — unless you let it.

Don't give up on life because you think you have run out of time. You won't run out of time until the moment your Soul decides to leave this earth. Until then, you literally have all the time in the world to do everything you want.

For the next week, I want you to track your time and what you are doing during your waking hours. You can download a copy of a time tracker at www.harmeschkaur.com.

For each hour you are awake, write down the activity you are doing. It doesn't matter if it is a meal, working in your job, or collecting the children from school. Whatever it is, write it down (time to get honest again!). And don't leave out things like watching Netflix or scrolling through social media!

Once the week is over, take a look at your tracker. Review how you spent your time and slot your activities into broad categories (e.g., eating, entertainment, errands, etc.).

1. Tally the number of hours you spent on the activities in each category. Does anything shock or surprise you?

2. What activities are you doing that are simply filling time? These include

230

watching Netflix, scrolling through social media, and searching random things on the Internet.

3. What activities would you like to do if you had more time?

4. What activities would you be able to remove or reduce to give you more time to do the things you want?

Once you have these answers, you can start changing how you spend your time. This can include:

- Introducing small or significant changes in your routine

- Waking up earlier or staying up later

- Removing certain tasks altogether

- Adding new activities to your schedule, like that evening class you've wanted to take.

- Spending your time exactly how you want to is possible!

Exercises like the above help you make different and informed choices about where and how to spend your time.

IMPATIENCE

When was the last time you set an intention or declared that you wanted to achieve something, kept pushing to see immediate results, and became impatient? How did that work out for you?

As society has evolved, we have become more impatient. We want to see instant results, or we want to have our desires delivered right away. And in some areas of our life, that can happen. If you ordered this book online, chances are you received it relatively quickly. Same with clothes, housewares, groceries, and fast food. Society is quickly becoming able to deliver nearly everything we want in less and less time. But, even though those things may be seen as saving us time, they also promote the idea that we don't have time.

Take food delivery services. You've finished work on a Friday night and have plenty of food in the refrigerator, but you're just not in the mood for cooking and want something quick. So you reach for your phone and scroll through the handy food delivery app's at your fingertips. You spend a good ten to fifteen minutes deciding what to have and then order. Your wait time is over sixty minutes (it is Friday night, after all), but you are patient enough to wait for this under the false assumption that it's saving you time.

What if you had actually cooked the food you had? You probably would've finished eating and cleared up by the time your food from the delivery app reached you. And you would have saved money. Sometimes these time-saving apps aren't saving us time at all. It's the same with online clothes shopping. We think we are saving time by not getting in our cars, going to the shopping centre, and buying what we need. Let's order it to home, but then it comes, and it's not suitable or doesn't fit or look like it did in the picture. So now you have to arrange a return and look for something else. Which could mean driving into town and to the post office, or even worse, to the shopping centre to return in-store to the same place you could've gone in the first place!

You may be under the assumption that you are saving time, and in some cases, you may be, but where are you then spending that time you have saved? Is it to do something that moves you forward in creating the life you want to live, or is it spent on other mindless activities?

The same happens when we hyper-focus on a goal to the point that we start to lack patience. Say you want to work on your fitness and decide to join a gym. You may know what you want to achieve and the time frame to get there. But it might take longer than you'd hoped, or you have a slight slip-up or get an injury that slows your progress. When we come up against instances and challenges like this, it makes us want to give up. And believe me, many people do. But if this is a change you wish to be part of your new life, it is essential to view these occurrences as setbacks and carry on regardless. Because your goal *will* be achieved; it just may take a bit longer than you thought it would.

When people don't see or get the desired results as quickly as they want, they can get disheartened and decide not to go any further in their plans. This stops the plan altogether and blocks them from getting what they want. They may come back to it months or years later, but they've already blocked themselves by not having the patience to carry on with their plans.

I've learned from receiving coaching that my breakthrough will be on the other side of my lack of patience. When I started my coaching business, I watched fellow coaches sign clients and bring big money into their businesses, but it wasn't happening that way for me. I increased my presence on social media. I refined my messaging. I did everything I was coached to do, but I was impatient. I wanted things to happen as quickly as they were happening for others, and that impatience nearly led to me giving up multiple times. But I didn't give up, because I had the support of my fellow coaches and friends. They encouraged me to be patient and carry on. And they were right because pushing through gave me what I wanted in my business. If I had stopped, I would've blocked myself from creating the life I wanted. It would have prevented me from working for myself like I wanted to.

So, the takeaway here is this: Don't lose focus on what you set out to achieve because of a setback. Have patience because your breakthrough is just on the other side of the hard work you've already done.

Think back to past plans or goals that didn't quite work out as you wanted them to. Contemplate the following:

1. How long did you persevere before you gave up?

2. What was the reason that made you give up?

3. What support did you have when you were trying to reach your goal?

4. Have you gone back to that goal? If yes, what did you or are you doing differently this time to ensure success?

LACK OF SELF-BELIEF

Many people let a lack of self-belief create a barrier to the life they want. Instead of believing that we can achieve what we want, we might tell ourselves that good things only come to others. And then we sit and watch as others achieve their goals. Sounds like a self-fulfilling prophecy, doesn't it?

In Chapter 5, I referred to the Universe as a YES button. Whatever you ask from the Universe, it will give you. If you continually tell yourself that you can't achieve certain goals or that you can't have specific things, the Universe will agree, as if to say, 'Yes, you are right. You can't have what you want and won't achieve that goal.'

This can expand into how we see the world around us. Our internal thoughts start to create our external world. The more we see ourselves as unable to achieve what we want, the more we will see this perspective spill into multiple areas of the daily world around us.

This lack of self-belief affects many of us, so where does it stem from? I believe we can trace it back to learned behaviour and from others, especially caregivers from our early years, projecting their own lack of self-belief onto us.

When we are repeatedly told no as children, it embeds itself into our brains to the point where we don't ask anymore because we know the answer. We also see those around us trying to achieve certain things and experiencing knockbacks. And because of their lack of self-belief or lack of conviction, they give up. That shows us that if we initially fail at something, there is no point in continuing, and we may as well give up. Or, seeing this, we may decide never to start because why would we want to go through something only to fail?

I remember being in my teens and constantly being told, 'We can't afford it,' whenever I asked for something. It didn't matter whether it was something for school or myself. I heard those four words more times than I want to remember. Of course, there was a reason for it. I had younger siblings whose needs took priority over the 'unnecessary' things I wanted. I understand that now, but this taught me to adopt a scarcity mindset.

If you've read Chapter 8, you'll hear a bit about my story about money and debt. I don't think it was ever a coincidence that I had a lot of debt. My money stories started with those four words: 'We can't afford it.' For a long time, I believed I would never have enough money and would always struggle to earn the money I needed. This belief kept me in jobs that weren't well paid. It made me wonder what the point was of trying to get better-paid jobs because I still wouldn't get the amount of money I needed to support myself. I never seemed to be able to get myself out of this downward spiral — until I started listening to and observing people who were making more money.

What were they doing?

How were they doing it?

How were they setting themselves up for success?

As I've mentioned in this book, I didn't go to University, but there were plenty of vocational on-the-job training courses at my disposal. I started to apply for some of these opportunities. There wasn't any harm in trying, was there? I had to get comfortable knowing I might fail, but failing was okay. Not everything in my life had to be a success. And whatever was meant to be would be. I had to shift my mindset and learn to take risks where I hadn't done so before. I got better-paid jobs and on-the-job training that enabled me to apply for even better paid jobs. I learned new behaviours from my colleagues, managers, and peers. All this helped me create a new set of beliefs about myself and improve my self-belief.

Remember, there may be roadblocks or someone telling you that you are on the wrong path, or you will have to work extra hard to get to where you want to be. These things could stop you from creating the life you want and are there to keep you small.

If you want something, go for it. You can get it. Don't let others talk you out of it. They usually do this because they can't do it for themselves. You are not them; you are YOU. And you deserve the life you want. Remember what you learned about your Treasure Chest in Chapter 2.

Believe in the Universe, the gifts it has for you, and in yourself. With this triple-threat combo, no one will shake you, and you will be able to achieve everything you have dreamed of.

I haven't added an exercise here for you, as Chapter 8 features various exercises around money and how you currently view it.

LACK OF BOUNDARY SETTING

Like many people, my coaching clients share their difficulty with boundary setting. Some don't even realise a boundary is needed, but they're experiencing an increasingly frustrating or annoying situation. When they finally identify that a boundary is needed, they can put it and keep it in place to minimise annoyance or frustration.

Like other blocks discussed in this chapter, boundary setting can be hard to implement because it may not have been sufficiently modelled for us. Perhaps you were raised to always be available to others, no matter the demand or request. Before we realise it, life has become one long conveyor belt of other peoples' wants, dreams, and desires. And we happily pluck them off and attend to them without a second thought. Over time, this can leave us resentful, tired, frustrated, and angry. It might even leave us questioning our worth, wondering if our only purpose is caring for others' needs.

But it's not just boundaries with others that can cause us concern. It seems we increasingly don't have boundaries with ourselves; I've seen this more and more as technology rules our lives. We answer messages straight away because it has become an automatic reaction. We spend more time scrolling through social media, and we can shop instantaneously from our phones.

We aren't just on our phones when we are alone. We are also on our phones when we meet up with people in real life, and rather than being present, we drift in and out of conversations, causing fractured connections. We aren't enjoying the moment because we are documenting what we are doing, who we are with, and how much fun we are having.

When I'm out with friends or family, I want to be in their presence. I don't want to watch them scrolling through their phones or answering messages from people who aren't there. This is one of my biggest bugbears. I had a friend who, whenever we would meet up, would spend nearly the entire time on their phone. They would either be checking social media for what was going on elsewhere or answering messages from people they would have spoken to later. Once, they were so engrossed in their phone that I actually left them sitting in a bar and went for a thirty-minute walk around the block. When I returned, they hadn't even realised I'd been gone.

If you are not present in the here and now and in your own life, how will you even begin to be able to create it? You are already elsewhere, and that still isn't where you want your dream life to be.

Here's another thought about self-regulating boundaries: When you look at different areas of your life, are you where you want to be, or would some personal boundary setting improve these areas?

Let's say you've long wanted to take your family on a luxury holiday but haven't managed to save the money, disappointing your family and yourself.

What is your boundary around money? You will need to implement a suitable boundary to meet your goal. Look at where and how you're spending money. If you're spending disposable income on unnecessary items, you won't be saving for that luxury holiday. You will, in fact, be taking money away from that goal. You must set boundaries for how you and your family spend money until you've saved enough for your vacation. This will involve short-term sacrifices, but you'll reach your goal more quickly.

Or take the goal of wanting to eat more nutritious food. Look at why you are still eating food that isn't nutritious. Is it because you still allow junk food to be part of your weekly shopping? Is it because you need to learn to cook a wider variety of meals, so you don't always eat the same thing?

For everything we say we want to change in our lives, there is usually a personal boundary that we are not putting in place that enables us to make that change. It's not always because of outside influences. Sometimes we are our worst enemies in creating the lives we want. We don't like to acknowledge that we are the root of the problem! But once we create those boundaries, we can start living the way we desire.

5 Steps To Boundary Setting

Boundary setting is directly tied to your Sacred No and saying yes to yourself. Sometimes a situation needs only a minor adjustment in behaviour; however, problems like bullying, abuse of any kind, and other toxic behaviours require a deeper, more direct level of boundary setting.

I want to raise something that doesn't always sit well with my clients: *You* are accountable for your boundaries, and this ties back to taking responsibility for your life.

I've found that most of the time, stressful situations or people's poor behaviour toward you continue because *you* are allowing it to continue rather than addressing it and eliminating it from your life. So, your responsibility requires you to:

1. Identify where a boundary is needed.

2. Decide what the boundary needs to be.

3. Put the boundary in place.

4. Communicate the boundary.

5. Keep the boundary in place.

Let's look at each of these steps:

1. Identify where a boundary is needed.

This first step should be relatively easy for you. Look at the areas of your life and identify situations where you feel resentful, frustrated, or angry. Include instances that raise your stress levels or bring a sense of obligation.

Is your teenager not pulling their weight around the home? Is a work colleague making unreasonable demands of your time? How about the parent of one of your child's school friends always asking for a favour? Nothing and no one is off limits.

2. Decide what the boundary needs to be.

Once you have identified a situation that requires a boundary, you get to decide what the boundary for that situation needs to be. It could be as simple as asking someone to arrange a time with you rather than just showing up unannounced.

I recall a former colleague coming to me for guidance in their work tasks. At first, I was happy to help out, but after a while, the requests became more involved and technical to the point where I was falling behind in my own work to help them. I knew I needed to put a boundary in place.

I offered to arrange more targeted training with our manager and requested that this colleague set meetings with me with a clear agenda and outcomes to best use our time. These boundaries were effective, but there were still times when I had to say no to protect my time and work.

3. Put the boundary in place.

This step can feel tricky. You've identified the situation needing the boundary, but how do you implement it?

The answer is simple if the boundary is about your own behaviour, like making sure you don't look at your phone whilst at family gatherings. Discipline yourself to put your phone away; no one else needs to be involved in making this decision. (But if you repeatedly break your own rule, you may need to ask someone close to you to hold you accountable.)

Let's go back to the example of wanting to eat more healthy food. I've struggled with a sweet tooth, and when grocery shopping online, I'd add sweet treats along with whatever nutritious food I was buying. It had become an automatic habit. Going cold turkey wasn't easy either, so I had to put realistic boundaries in place to reduce my consumption of these treats to the point where I was able to eliminate them from my online grocery orders.

Boundaries involving only you are relatively easy to set, but when your boundary involves ensuring someone else's behaviour no longer impacts you, let's move to the next step.

4. Communicate the boundary.
There is no simple way to say this. If someone else is negatively impacting you with their behaviour, you have no choice but to talk to them about it. That is the only way to honestly communicate a boundary.

This may scare the heck out of you, and it's understandable. You could send an email, but the recipient might ignore or misinterpret it. Some might suggest that you take more aggressive action, like removing the offending person from your life or avoiding them. This approach is necessary if their behaviour endangers you in any way. But I know from experience that speaking to someone face to face about their behaviour is the best option, even if you don't get the desired result.

Anything short of this direct approach always left me feeling that there was unfinished business, always wondering if the other person would contact me after I pressed send on an email that should have been a live conversation. Do you want to spend your life looking over your shoulder, waiting for this person and their bad behaviour to come back into your life?

It's never fun to confront someone about their bad behaviour, but you will feel empowered and proud of yourself when you do it. Challenging yourself to have these conversations also helps you see if this behaviour is really bothering you or if you need to examine something within yourself more closely.

5. Keep the boundary in place.

This step is sometimes the hardest one. You've identified and communicated your boundaries, and now you have to live up to what you've asked for. Letting others cross your boundaries shows you're not serious and that your words are empty. It also encourages others to continue their bad behaviour, reigniting the cycle.

None of us is perfect, so there will be slip-ups, especially when you feel unsure. That's human nature, and it's okay. Don't beat yourself up over it, as this could lead to your giving up on the boundary altogether. When you're back to your confident high-vibe self, it will be easier to enforce your limits.

Knowing your personality type can help you understand how you interact with people and how to best set healthy boundaries. I am an ambivert, someone who is an extroverted introvert. Susan Cain's book, *Quiet: The Power of Introverts in a World That Won't Stop Talking*, has helped me understand my energy. To best utilise it, I had to create boundaries with myself and others to shape my life. Once I set those boundaries and exercised my Sacred No, certain people started dropping off my radar. It was natural, and they didn't contact me as much. They moved on with their lives, freeing up my time and energy to direct toward nurturing positive changes in my life.

I do want to add a note here about boundaries that other people set. Just as it is acceptable for you to set boundaries for yourself and express them to others, others are able to do the same. And this in itself can feel uncomfortable. We must also accept that others are within their rights and standards to say no to us or disagree with our behaviours. Some people may find us uncompromising, and it's perfectly okay for them to feel this way and express this to us if they are creating their own boundaries.

It is all about respect for one another and how we choose to create and live our lives.

Creating boundaries has been one of the most impactful tools in cultivating a life I love. I still go along with other people and their plans sometimes, but it is a rarity rather than a regular occurrence — and it is always my choice. Boundaries have helped me foster balance in my life, and I wish this for you too.

1. Identify two or three areas of your life where you think implementing boundaries would benefit you.

2. Using the steps I have outlined, make a plan to put those boundaries in place. It can take time but notice what happens when the boundary is put in place. Is there resistance from others to what you are doing or proposing?

3. Notice how you feel as you act on your plan. It will help you see where there may be more work to be done in raising your

confidence or where you are much more assertive than you think!

NOT EXERCISING OUR POWER OF CHOICE

We all have the power of choice. Some people may not believe that, but we do. Every single one of us. So why do we feel we don't have a choice or 'have' to do something?

I remember a particular Friday morning when I was still in my 9-to-5 job. I woke up thinking, 'Thank God it's Friday!' It had been a challenging work week, to the point where the day before, after a meeting with a more senior colleague, I screamed into a cushion. I'm not over-exaggerating.

My job frustration had reached an all-time high. Our project team leaders had brushed my team's concerns aside for the past eighteen months. After that Thursday call, I reached a point where I needed to scream. Thank you, pandemic, because I wouldn't have been able to do that in the office!

Even with this, I didn't resign. I was close to doing so, but I chose not to at that moment because I had a bigger plan. I had a sequence of events that needed to take place before I could resign, and it was already in motion. Even though I felt immense frustration at that job, I chose to stay. I'm lucky because my choice came from an informed place.

Some people don't always make their choices from informed places. How often have you wanted to quit an unfulfilling job, only to have your nearest and dearest remind you how lucky you are to have a job? Enduring just a few of their fear-based questions may have you wondering if you really want to quit or if you're just being dramatic. It was just one bad day at work, right?

And there it is. We choose to stay in a place that doesn't serve us. I'm talking about a job because it is where we spend most of our waking hours, but this can apply to any area of your life. You have a choice, but you have to exercise that choice.

Let's return to my former job situation for a moment. I was a contractor for about ten years. Before that, I was a permanent employee because I believed a permanent role meant good career progression, salary rises, and bonuses. But when I discovered that contractors on my team were getting paid a lot more than me and doing the same or less work, it drove me to choose to be a contractor. And it was an excellent choice for me! I shook off my beliefs that I wouldn't be able to get a mortgage or have job security — the two biggest reasons that had kept me in a permanent role.

And guess what? They weren't even true! As a contractor, I secured a mortgage for a flat I bought in London. And as for job security? I haven't had a break from my work since I was sixteen.

My former beliefs informed my choices. But if our beliefs are not accurate or we've learned them from other people, are we really making the right choices for us?

Your life is your life, and you are your number one priority. Your choices — good or bad — seep into every area and impact those around you. The point is that YOU get to choose. When you're connected with yourself and don't make your choices from a place of people-pleasing or a need for validation, your choices will start to bring change and benefit to you as you've never seen before.

1. Where in your life do you feel you haven't
    had a choice?

2. What was the outcome of having a lack of
    choice?

3. What would you have done or chosen
    differently if you were given permission to
    do what you wanted?

4. If you could do so now, would you change your choice?

5. Look at the people around you who you think are making good choices. What about them inspires you to create different or better choices?

NOT TAKING BACK YOUR POWER

What does it mean to take back your power? How we navigate the challenges in our lives shows us where our power is. If we proactively tackle and resolve that challenge quickly and efficiently, we have managed to stand in our power. Unfortunately, many of us wait for something outside of us to happen before we change our lives.

What do I mean by this?

- Say you're in a job you don't particularly enjoy. You've been feeling this way for quite a while, but you decide to see what your salary rise or bonus will be before you decide to find another job.

- Or maybe you're in a long-term relationship but don't see it progressing. You decide to wait until your partner frustrates you to the point where you have no choice but to leave.

- Or maybe you're in a toxic friendship, where the other person drains your energy and only takes rather than gives, and you are deciding to spend

> less time with that person rather than end the friendship.

You are not holding on to your power in these situations; you are giving your control to the other person or situation. You are waiting for something to happen in those relationships, so you don't have to decide to do something about them. Does this sound familiar?

You could wait a long time if you want someone else to decide for you. Let's review that hypothetical job situation. You already know that you don't particularly like your job and no longer want to work there. But you want to wait and see how your employer compensates you before you make a decision. You may have short-term satisfaction if you get the salary rise or bonus you want, but where does that leave you once it is absorbed into your daily life? You will most likely still not enjoy your job.

I've experienced this in jobs where I wasn't fulfilling my potential and didn't like my environment. Simply put, the money kept me there. Until the financial crash in 2009, salary raises and bonuses in the industry I worked in were pretty good. But as soon as the crash happened, it gave employers the excuse to cut back because it wouldn't look good to be paying out money to staff when so much money had been lost by financial institutions. That excuse continues to be used today; only now, the global pandemic and rising costs are the excuse.

When this money dried up, you'd think I would just leave, wouldn't you? Wrong! I stayed a few more years, hoping my salary would increase in line with my workload, but it didn't. I gave away my power to my employer when I should have moved on. And it's not about not feeling appreciated by our employers. Some of us have passions and dreams that we are worried about leaving our jobs to pursue. We become very comfortable working for others and having a regular income rather than branching out and trying out alternative work for ourselves.

It's the same in relationships. Perhaps we reach a stage where our partner can no longer provide what we need or want in a relationship. Instead of talking with them and potentially causing them hurt, we remain quiet. Maybe you've seen friends construct situations where they push their partner to a point where the partner decides to leave the relationship, giving them a way out they didn't want to take for themselves. Why spend time unhappy, waiting on someone else's timeline to end the relationship, when you could bite the bullet and make the change now?

The pandemic taught us how short life is. Many people used the situation to utilise their power and make life-changing decisions. They resigned from jobs they didn't enjoy, left relationships that were no longer serving them, spent time with people they enjoyed, set up businesses, and pursued their passions. They took their power back from the trappings and pressures of society today.

I've witnessed friends follow their passions, work on their self-development, and take steps to live in a different way than they did pre-pandemic. Not one of them (including me) regrets taking those steps. They have a greater sense of who they are, what they like (and don't like), and who they want to be in this world.

I've also seen people stay in their comfort zones, toxic situations, and uncomfortable realities, despite their declarations of wanting to change and do something different. Even the pandemic that stirred something in so many others to live differently couldn't seem to wake these Souls.

1. Think about a time when a specific situation in your life changed, but it wasn't

down to your choices. Think about where your power was and whether you were holding your power or whether you had given it to someone else. What was the situation? What would you do differently to protect and keep your own power in that situation?

2. Imagine a friend coming to you about a challenge or situation they are in. What advice would you give them? Would you tell them to wait out the situation or encourage them to take action and stand in their power?

FEAR OF GETTING WHAT WE WANT

Imagine you're on the brink of an amazing goal: studying hard to pass an exam, seeing gains at the gym, or dating someone who feels perfect for you. Then all of a sudden, this goal starts slipping out of reach. You stop studying so hard, cut back on gym sessions, or ghost the person who seems to fit so perfectly into your life.

What is happening? It was all going so well! You were nearly there at the place where your dreams were about to come true. Why walk away from all you've wanted?

Some of us have a fear of success and getting what we want. Yes, that's right. It's not the fear of failure; it's the fear of actually succeeding in what we've wanted for so long. This may seem a bit counterproductive. Didn't you start studying, working out, or dating so that you could succeed somehow? The closer we get to our goal, our old patterns of thinking and behaving pop back up to remind us we're not worthy of what we're about to attain. They tell us that even if we get what we want, we'll just mess up, proving our efforts were pointless. Sound familiar?

When we get used to things not working out, we start believing this will happen in every situation in our life. We panic when it looks like we might actually get what we desire. What if you get what you want? What then? What does life look like after that?

Our learned behaviours and experiences keep us striving to get what we want but falling short. Like competing with one arm tied behind us, it becomes exhausting! And that's when some people give up. They decide they want a comfortable, easy life and stop striving. They create a reality they can deal with day in and day out without much thought or challenge.

You wouldn't be alone in thinking or behaving this way. I've fallen victim to this self-sabotaging behaviour, knowing I'm on the edge of something great, but something would stop me from going the extra mile to reach the goal. The idea of leaving people behind stopped me. If I created the life I wanted, not everyone could come along. Was I ready for that? What if things didn't work out, and I made changes for nothing?

Some of my mentors would often ask, 'But what if it did work out?' We allow ourselves to play out all the ways something won't work out, and we forget to let ourselves play out how something *will* work.

This phenomenon isn't quite like the fear we might have of flying or spiders, but it can definitely paralyse us on the path we set ourselves on. To gain something great, we often must give up something not so great. Unfortunately, that not-so-great thing can have a hold over us that can't be explained.

Until we delve deeper to learn what that is, we'll always reach that point just before greatness. We desire a better life, but when it shows up for us, it may scare us because it doesn't look exactly how we pictured it. Here's the secret: It is usually even better than we imagined.

'But I don't feel ready! I don't feel deserving.'

'Who am I to live this wonderful, joyful, exciting life?'

'Why have I been chosen to walk this path instead of someone else who also needs to make big changes?'

Don't let messages like this stand in your way. Remember, this type of life is available to everyone, and everything we have ever wanted is already in our Treasure Chests. But to get there, we must meet the challenges and obstacles before us. Why? Because it will show how much we really want the life our Souls are here to live.

Try and think of a time when you were so close to the finishing line of a goal, but you didn't manage to get to where you thought you wanted to be. Perhaps it was a job opportunity or a money-saving goal, or a fitness goal. Self-sabotage is a great way for us to stop getting to the place we dream of.

In what ways do you find yourself sabotaging your dreams? For example, it could be allowing yourself to stay in bed on a rainy day rather than making the trip to the gym. Maybe it is allowing yourself to buy an outrageously expensive gift for a friend rather than downsizing the present and saving money towards that holiday you want to go on.

What could you do or put in place to limit your self-sabotaging behaviours?

WAITING FOR 'PERFECT' CONDITIONS

Have you ever stalled on making a change because you wanted to 'feel ready'? It's easy to use the idea of everything being perfectly in place before we act as an excuse. You and I both know that life doesn't work that way. If we waited until everything was perfect, we would never do anything about our situation.

Hear this: You will never be ready to make a big change. Your life is not going to wait for you. You have to start to see the opportunities and challenges coming your way and take them when they are in front of you.

Yes, there are certain situations, like purchasing a home, where you must have pieces of the puzzle in place before taking action. You need to have a deposit, the finances for the move, solicitor's fees, etc. It would be pretty disappointing if you found the perfect place but didn't have the finances, meaning you can move more quickly when you find your new home.

When I talk about being ready, it has more to do with our behaviours and attitudes:

- I'll launch that podcast once I have more confidence or technical skills.

- I'll join the gym once I lose a few pounds and won't feel as embarrassed working out in front of others.

- I'll entertain friends once I've learned to cook.

Do any of these sound familiar? What's stopping you from doing those things right now? Because really, there are no physical barriers to starting a podcast, joining a gym, hosting a dinner party, or (fill in the blank).

Confidence grows through doing. It's not something we are all born with. Our conditioning can affect our confidence, but the only way to build it up is to do the thing we want to do. I remember when I first started coaching. I'd participated in coaching programmes telling me I needed to 'put myself out there' on social media. As someone who didn't even like taking selfies, this brought up a lot of fear and made me feel physically sick! It resurfaced all the childhood memories of not being liked and being teased at school. What if I showed myself on social media and people started to tease me? I didn't think I could handle that.

My wonderful coach at the time challenged me to show up on my social media account and talk to my audience in real time or pre-recorded. I didn't feel ready and wanted to make sure I had make-up and nice clothes on, plus time to practice what to say. My coach suggested I let people see me as myself, not some perfect side of myself, because that is what people relate to.

It took a couple of days to bring myself to do it. I was out for a walk, and even as I was looking and speaking to the camera, I felt stupid and self-conscious as other people walked by. I uploaded my video to my social media account, and all I could think was that people would not be nice about it. I felt fake doing it and that I would come across as so. My confidence in creating this video was slowly starting to disappear. But then I had numerous people reaching out and celebrating me for having done it. They related to what I'd shared, making them want to do something equally daring for themselves.

It still took me a while to get comfortable showing up on social media videos, and it wasn't until I was in another coaching programme that the game changed for me. This programme issued a ten-day challenge to show up on video talking about a controversial subject each day to my audience.

That challenge helped me get comfortable and showed me how to reach out to people and connect differently. It also helped me to practice and gain confidence. I wasn't ready, but I had to jump in and take a risk because what was the alternative? Never share my message? Never connect with the people I was trying to help?

As a coach, it is about people investing in you. If people relate to you and like what they see, they will hire you or, at the very least, get on a call to see what you're all about. If I hid behind posts and didn't show up the way I did, I wouldn't be able to connect in the way I do. I wasn't ready, but I just had to jump in and learn along the way.

And that's what some of us are not prepared to do. We want our situation to be perfect before we make the jump to the life we want. When we take the risk, even when we don't feel ready, our growth makes the end goal even sweeter because we've challenged our past behaviours and thinking.

You will never be ready, so what is the point of waiting? It really is time to take the leap.

1. Write down three things that you would like to do but feel some fear about doing.

2. What do you feel you need to do to be 'ready' to do the things you've listed?

3. What is the one action you could take today that would start you on the path of the things you've listed?

Now go out and do it!

COMPARISON & JEALOUSY

Have you heard the expression, 'Comparison is the thief of joy?' Comparing ourselves to others and what they have drains our energy in untold ways. When you are creating this new life for yourself, I urge you to please be cautious of comparison.

I think it's perfectly okay to look at someone else's life for inspiration, but if we start comparing what we have to the point where it never feels like enough, we can get ourselves into a heap of trouble!

Creating our life needs to come from a place of wonder and curiosity rather than thinking we'll be happier if we have a particular thing. More often than not, that thing won't make us happy because it's not what we really want. We saw that someone else had it and were happy, so we did the same. That is their path and their life. Ours can look very different.

Comparing ourselves to others can leave us feeling bad about ourselves — and that kind of energy will not attract anything good into our lives. In fact, it will block us from receiving all the goodness that is out there for us. When we are stuck in a negative comparison cycle, the good stuff just isn't getting to us.

And this isn't just about material things. It's about you as a person. Are you comparing yourself to someone you think has the life you want? Are you trying to change yourself into them to live that life?

We have to be ourselves to create the life we want to live. Yes, we all evolve and change over time, but we remain ourselves, just a different and (hopefully) better version. Taking on other people's personality traits because we think that will help us create the life we want is not being true to ourselves.

I've mentioned in this book about my relationship with the gym and how my mindset has changed over time. When I was a gym bunny, my interest in working out came from a place of comparison. I wanted a romantic partner at the time, and from what I had seen in the relationships around me, I would only find a partner if my body looked a certain way. I compared myself to other women in relationships and tried to act and dress like them. And guess what? I did have the opportunity to have romantic partners.

But those opportunities were based on me trying to be someone else. It was never me; I was still trying to fit in with others and be what I thought they wanted me to be instead of simply being myself. I didn't always feel comfortable, which led to drinking more to relax and make it through nights out — all because I thought I had to be a certain way to attract a romantic partner!

But this kind of game wasn't limited to one area of my life. It showed up everywhere:

Was I good enough at my job?

Was where I lived good enough?

Was I earning enough?

Were other people earning more than me?

The comparison never ended. I tried to live the life of other people, not my own life. I aimed to show up in the world as other people, not as myself. How could I create an authentic life when all I was doing was copying a life that other people were living?

This is why it is essential to look at where our desires come from. Are they genuinely coming from us for our highest good and for that better version of ourselves? Or are they coming from a place of comparison and jealousy?

 ACTIVATION

Comparison is not easy to acknowledge or be aware of because we would like to think that the decisions we make are of our own doing and not because we see something in someone else. I want you to be as honest as possible with yourself when considering the questions below.

What was the last thing you did because you have seen someone else do it, and it worked out for them? For example, maybe a family member or friend relocated abroad and managed to uplevel their life, and you decided to do it too because it seemed like the perfect antidote to your own situation.

How did that situation work out for you?

274

Knowing what you do now, would you still make that same decision? Why or why not?

AGE

As we go through life, we can become comfortable with what we do and how we live. And the older we become, the harder it can be for us to make changes.

As I was growing up, if you weren't settled down with at least one child on the way by the time you were in your mid-twenties, you were already considered behind in life. The societal, prescribed life of being born, going to school, pursuing further education, getting a job, meeting someone, and settling down to have children and a house and car is a path many take.

Thankfully in today's world, if you haven't done all of this by the time you reach your mid-thirties, you are still considered on the right path. It is more acceptable now to go through a period of exploration and experimentation in your twenties to better understand what you want from your life.

Even with more relaxed attitudes, many of us still feel that when we get to a certain age, we cannot change things and must accept what we have and live out the rest of our days in this way. It'll come as no surprise to you then that I'm going to tell you this isn't true!

It's no wonder that people go through existential crises! Most of us are raised to believe in a particular way of life, and when we don't achieve that, we wonder what is missing, where we are going wrong, and what our life purpose is if we're not following the prescribed path.

You can change your life at any age and stage. There is no rule book, apart from the one in our heads, that tells us when we can do certain things. If you want to start a business in your fifties, go for it! If you wish to return to university for a degree in your forties, just do it! Nothing can stop you from doing anything in your life but you.

I didn't follow the path most people in my culture do. I am still single and nearly fifty years old as I write this. I was in my mid-forties when I realised I get to choose how I live my life. I get to create what I want — not anyone else.

I had been limiting myself because of my age, thinking that I would have to remain in a 9-to-5 job until retirement age and, until then, try to fill up my life with activities to pass the time. I thought I was too old to start a new career.

Around the time I worked for the Australian company (mentioned earlier in this book), I realised my life didn't have to go the way society kept telling me it had to. I was working, but it wasn't in the standard 9-to-5 way others were working. My days opened up to let me explore different things and work on myself. It gave me time to think about how I wanted my life to be. I knew then that I didn't want to still work in a corporate job by the time I was fifty.

I knew I wanted to work towards a career or job that would let me work on my schedule. I wanted to be my own boss, and I told myself it wasn't too late to start working on it. My age had nothing to do with it. It was a choice I had to make. Did I want to stay living the same way that I was, or did I want to create a lifestyle for myself that I enjoyed waking up to every single day? You know which one I chose!

I want you to think about the people you know, family, friends, and colleagues. Specifically, people who are in their forties and older.

1. Out of all of these people, who is inspiring to you and why?

2. What have they done or are doing that makes you want to change things up in your life?

3. What things have you stopped yourself from doing because you felt your age influenced your decision? Do you still feel this is true?

PROCRASTINATION

We think we have all the time in the world to do what we want, which means many of us put off doing things because we believe we can do them later.

Tomorrow is another day! It's okay if I didn't get around to it today because I can do it tomorrow, next week, next month, or (insert time frame).

Even though we think we don't have enough hours in the day to do the things we have to, we will still put off what we want to do. But sadly, for some of us, that time will not come.

I've heard stories of people who worked hard their entire lives, building up their savings, only to find themselves diagnosed with a long-term illness or incurable disease that kept them from enjoying retirement. I'm sure you've heard stories like this too.

Before I finally took the leap to work as a full-time coach and writer, my last corporate role was for a financial institution. My colleague Sue always worked hard, coming in early, helping colleagues out, and giving her all. When the pandemic hit in 2020, Sue decided to retire early to spend time with her husband and family. She knew life can be short, and she wanted to enjoy it. At the time of writing this book, in 2022, our team learned that Sue had been diagnosed with an inoperable brain tumour, and she only had six weeks to live. I was devastated for her, knowing that she'd had plans to travel and see parts of the world she loved. The world had been closed to travel due to the pandemic and it was slowly starting to open again. I'm not sure she managed to travel as she had hoped, but I trust she managed to enjoy her life until her journey on earth ended.

I've written a lot in this book about how many of us are taught to follow a prescribed life path, that if we put in long years of hard work, we're rewarded with time to do the things we've desired for so long. Stories like Sue's remind us that not all of us get to do so.

More and more young people are not living by the rules that those of us forty years and over seem to live by, and it makes me happy that they aren't! They don't have to have a 9-to-5 job if that isn't what they want. Even though some jobs are becoming obsolete because of automation, different job roles have been created that play to the younger generation's talents, skills, and ingenuity.

These young adults aren't happy working until later in life to finally enjoy themselves. They are enjoying themselves now. They're working in ways that mean they can travel and work simultaneously. They're not tied down to one location in the world for forty-eight weeks of the year, only venturing outside of this when they have paid holidays. They are doing work they enjoy, which doesn't feel like work. It has become their life, a life they enjoy.

We could take a leaf out of their books. We don't just get to learn from the older generations, but the younger generations are here to teach us something too.

Do not wait until you are older to create the life you want to live.

Start building that life now.

Do the things you want to do.

Experience everything that you want to experience.

Do not put limits on yourself because you think you have to wait.

Newsflash: You don't.

The only person telling you that is you!

I want you to create a life you want to wake up to every day — one that fills you with joy so you can share that joy with others.

Before Sue passed away, she shared a message with her ex-colleagues (paraphrased): 'Go and live your life. Enjoy a glass of wine, and go out and have fun. That's what life is about. '

There are those of us who are fully aware that life can be short. We may not get to do everything we want because we know that time travels at warp speed. We have so many ideas of the life we want to live that it causes us to stop because we don't know which way to turn first. We suffer a form of paralysis because everything deserves our attention.

I have felt like this. When I was in the pit of my depression, I had very little hope for my future and what it could potentially look like. I wasn't worried about time; I only worried about getting through the day. Once I had hope and dreams again, it felt like time was running out. Even now, I sometimes feel that I won't be able to do everything I want to do or see everything I want to see because I don't know how long I have left on this earth. That makes me want to live every single day to the fullest of my ability. Shouldn't I then live life as I want to before my time runs out? Why would I want to spend time doing things I don't like or with people who aren't high on my priority list?

I'm sure you've considered what you would do if you were told you had only one week to live. Would you continue living the way you are now, or try to cram in as much fun, joy, and other good stuff? I bet it would be the latter. So why don't we do that now, whilst we are still here? What are we waiting for?

Life really is too short. I have only learned this as I've gotten older. And the funny thing is that I heard older people say the same thing when I was younger! They realised as they hit their fifties, sixties, and beyond that time doesn't wait around for anyone. NOW is the time to enjoy your life. It's a rite of passage we all seem to go through. We spend our early years believing we can put things off until we have more time and space in our lives. But when we get there, we realise we should have made the most of our time. And try telling that to a younger person! Whenever I heard that in my twenties, I brushed it aside as some rubbish older people liked to say. And now, I am saying the same thing to younger people!

I don't care how old you are. It's never too early or late to create the life you want to live. Have you ever heard the sayings 'Forty is the new thirty?' or 'Sixty is the new forty?' I have, and I believe it's because many of us have a younger outlook on life than past generations did. We take better care of ourselves and refuse to believe that life ends when we reach a certain age. In fact, we believe that life begins at certain ages! And that's because we have been growing up gathering knowledge and experience so that it can help us later in life.

Will there still be people in their sixties and seventies who walk the old path and don't look to change their lives? Absolutely, but I also know those who have experienced moments of profound clarity that only ageing can bring to grab hold of a new lease on life.

When I turned forty, I had a panic attack. It was the first panic attack I'd ever had, and I thought I was having a heart attack. I thought my life was over. I had gotten over the worst of my depression (or so I'd thought), and now my life was over because I turned forty. If only my future self had come back to tell me my life was about to truly begin and that I'd be able to put everything I'd learned so far into practice to create a life I wanted to live. Of course, that didn't happen, and I still had to walk my path until those realisations came.

Think about where you are in your life right now. Are there activities or goals you are putting off because you're waiting for something to happen (more money, more confidence, more skills, retirement)?

1. Write down the top three things you are putting off doing and why.

2. What would your life look like if you were to pursue those three things now in your current life?

3. Do you still want to put off doing those three things? Or are you inspired to take that next step?

THE FEAR OF LETTING GO

What would your answer be if I asked you how attached you are to things? There is no right or wrong answer here, but whatever you say will indicate how much you want to change your life. Material possessions are relatively easy to let go of unless they have sentimental value. How many things do you need to live your best life?

It can get more complicated with emotional and personal attachments, like the people in your life, the places you like to go, and your daily behaviours.

I've led many coaching sessions where a client wants to change, but something stops them. Even when they are shown the line that they must step over for that change to happen, something keeps them from doing so. They know their new, improved life is beyond the line, but they can't bring themselves to step over it and claim what's theirs.

Have you ever experienced that feeling?

Maybe your drinking habits are not allowing you to live the life you really want. Beyond the line is a life where drinking isn't an issue; you can take it or leave it. You are healthier and happier. Your relationships have improved, and you've found a job you are passionate about. But to step over that line, you have to give something up. And it's not just the physical act of drinking that needs to be kicked to the curb. There is something more profound to release.

This is where our friend Ego comes in and starts telling us all how stepping beyond that line would be the most terrible thing we will ever do. It reminds us why we need to keep drinking and tells us that everything will be okay if we stay on this side of the line and don't need to step to the other side.

This is where our limitations, learned and imposed, become very apparent.

This is where we start to believe what Ego is telling us.

This is where we stop ourselves from stepping over the line and continue our life in the way it has been serving us so far.

But...there is always a but. There *will* come a time when we walk up to that line again. It could be the very next day or weeks or months later. It could be years later, but we will step up to the line again and go through that same process.

We have an inbuilt fear of letting go of the things we do know to step into the things we don't know. We hold on to the limitations because they are safe and comforting. The unknown lies beyond the line, and we don't see what's there. We hope it's all the good things we think about and desire. It takes courage to step over that line into the unknown and the better version of your life.

We may also fear that once we step over this line, we'll never be able to go back. Maybe we believe we'll experience loss — and we will. We lose our old life and replace it with something new. We already know we want to change our lives and that how we live is no longer serving us. So, why would stepping over the line be a bad thing? It couldn't be any worse than where we are now.

Stepping into a newly created life also entails letting go of people, behaviours, locations, jobs, possessions, emotions, and attachments to move forward.

Take the drinking example again: If you want to give up drinking, but your friend group is centred around drinking, and that's what you do every time you all meet up, then you have a choice to make. Either you keep going out with that group of people and continue drinking, or you express your desire to stop drinking and suggest alternatives to going to the pub. You will soon discover who the real friends are who support you in this new way of life.

The fear could be losing a group of friends, which is natural. You've built up relationships with these people. It would be easier to keep going as usual, but the cycle will continue. After another horrendous hangover, you'll tell yourself you want to give up drinking and start a healthier way of life. You will come to the line again. It may take a few times before you step over, but you will, and then you will wonder why you hadn't done it sooner.

We may also fear that as we move forward and relationships change or are lost, we will not be thought kindly of. We inherently want to be liked, even by people we don't know. When we speak out about what we really want and start to make changes, the people around us may no longer be able to relate — and definitely not as they did before. Knowing this and being comfortable with it can determine how and when we move forward.

When I started to create my life from a conscious level, my choices to help me step forward brought me a level of sadness. I wanted to have conversations I knew I couldn't have with the current people in my life. I had a world inside me trying to get out, but I was scared because I didn't have anyone around me I could talk to about those things.

That changed when I met my online coaching community full of people doing the same self-development work I was. We shared similar interests, including wanting to embrace a profession that helped us bring about the same level of transformation in others that we'd experienced for ourselves.

Something unexpected also happened. Finding this new group of like-minded people made it harder to relate to those I'd known most of my life. We no longer shared the same interests. There was a time when I would have remained in the same zone as my old friends to keep some community and friendship alive and not be alone, but meeting new, positive people meant I didn't have to do that anymore.

I've had some of the most interesting conversations with the people I met online, during a pandemic, through a group coaching programme. (Trust me, my former self would never have thought it possible to write that sentence!) These people were creating extraordinary lives for themselves, hosting podcasts, writing books, and running mentorships and workshops. They inspire me to keep working on my own life and to call in the things that bring me joy and fulfilment.

Still, I had to limit my time with people who didn't bring the same positive energy into my life. I still talk to some of these colleagues and friends, but it is minimal and not how it used to be. It can feel sad and a bit like a breakup. People can naturally outgrow each other, which is precisely what happened.

I was outgrowing the people I had spent a lot of time with and was also moving beyond that version of me. If you can relate to this, I want to tell you that this is okay. It is normal. Some people may kick and scream as you start to live your newly created life because they don't see themselves in it. And you may feel guilty or sad knowing that you are going on to something better for yourself. But it really is okay.

It took me a while to come to terms with this, and when I realised it was the thing that was holding me back, I had no choice but to face it. I could choose Door #1 and stay in my old reality and remain resentful and frustrated — two of the primary emotions that made me want to change my life in the first place. Or I could choose Door #2 and feel a temporary sadness and guilt that would inevitably give way to happiness, fulfilment, joy, and freedom — all the emotions I wanted to feel — by letting go and devoting my life to helping myself and others.

You already know I chose Door #2. Which door will you choose?

This exercise is a bit like a stock take. Only it's in relation to your behaviours/traits that are perhaps holding you back.

1. Write down as many behaviours or traits that come to mind and that are more likely habitual rather than intentional. For example, eating healthy and nutritious meals during the week, only to revert to junk food at the weekends.

2. Which three of these behaviours or traits would you most like to change or eliminate?

3. What are these behaviours or traits holding you back from doing in your life?

4. What action do you plan to take to change these behaviours or traits?

FINAL THOUGHT

Maybe after reading this chapter, you're feeling overwhelmed and anxious, or wondering how you are ever going to be able to create the life you want for yourself with all of these blocks to contend with. Yes, there are a lot of blocks that I've covered here, and it's worth remembering that not all of them are going to apply to you. There may be a few that stand out more for you depending on where you are in your current life, and these can change as you grow and evolve.

I've created one last exercise for this chapter so that you can gather your thoughts and decide how you want to move forward.

The list of blocks covered in this chapter was:

- People pleasing
- Not saying yes to you
- The Sacred No
- Lack of time
- Impatience
- Lack of self-belief
- Lack of boundary setting
- Not exercising your power of choice
- Not taking back your power
- Fear of getting what you want
- Waiting for 'perfect' conditions
- Comparison and jealousy
- Age
- Procrastination
- The fear of letting go

1. From the list, which three blocks resonate most with where you are in your life right now?

2. How do these blocks show up in your everyday life?

3. What practices or tools could you use to remind you to keep working through these blocks so that it would get you to where you want to be in life?

CHAPTER TEN:
MENTAL HEALTH AND WELL-BEING

What mental health needs is more sunlight, more candour, and more unashamed conversation.

– Glenn Close

I WANT TO DEDICATE a short chapter to mental health and well-being because it once was the biggest barrier to living the life I wanted, and I don't want it to be an obstacle for you.

In my twenties, I felt anger, sadness, frustration, and a lack of hope or purpose. I worked in retail back then, and a colleague one day mentioned they thought I was depressed and encouraged me to seek help. Of course, my defences came up when they said it, but later on, I started to wonder if they were on to something. I had been in a 'mood' for about ten years, but puberty and growing up in a Sikh community where I saw other women in similar 'moods' made me believe it was all a part of adult life. I was very pessimistic about myself and other people; I just couldn't see the point of life.

My colleague's concerns prompted me to visit my doctor, who told me my problems would be solved with a better diet and exercise. I dutifully tried to follow my doctor's advice, hoping for a miracle, but it didn't help. When I pressed the issue again, I was offered six weeks of counselling which barely scratched the surface of my issues.

In fact, it opened up the chasm of the problems I hadn't been facing. I had to battle with my doctor and my local NHS Trust to be seen by a mental health professional and to be taken seriously. I increasingly had suicidal thoughts, partly due to the medication I'd been prescribed. I didn't want to live because if what I was doing was living, it certainly wasn't much fun. And eventually, after much advocating for myself, I spent eighteen months under the care of a mental health nurse and psychiatrist.

I write more about this experience in the Introduction, and that period allowed me to feel somewhat better and start building a happier life for myself. I had hope again that I could get a good job, that I wasn't a bad person who didn't deserve happiness, and that life wasn't so bad after all. And for a while, I did build that better life. But then I discovered the truth about my mental health: that the depression would always be there, waiting for something to trigger it and let it back out of its cage — and that's exactly what happened nearly ten years later.

Gary Speed was a famous professional footballer. One day it was announced in the news that he had taken his own life, and no one knew why. I didn't know him. He wasn't even a footballer at my favourite club, Arsenal, so he wasn't someone I had any inclination to think about. But I remember being on the tube to work the next day and feeling an immense wash of dread and panic. I got off at the next stop, taking deep breaths to calm myself down.

That's when I knew I'd never be rid of depression, and now anxiety had decided to come along for the ride. That one news story dragged me back to a dark place I thought I had left behind. Even now, years later, if this story is mentioned in the news or I see an article about Gary Speed, my body can't help but react. It remembers that day on the tube. Luckily, remembering is as far as it gets, but I also learned that if I didn't take care of myself, depression was only a short ride away.

During my second round of depression and anxiety, which I write about in Chapter 1, I was trying to hold onto the life I had been building. But the feeling of sadness, hopelessness, and panic led me to destructive behaviours that could have seen me lose everything. I spent several years in a cycle of drinking and nursing hangovers, choosing toxic relationships rather than those that would support me. I got to a point where I told myself I didn't want to be like this anymore. I couldn't continue to live like this because there would only be one outcome if I did. From the outside, I looked like everything in my life was great: a good job, a lovely flat, good friends, great social life. Inside I was unhappy, negative, lost, and didn't see the point of being alive. I had to change.

I found an amazing therapist and spent about eight months working with her. I was lucky enough to be able to pay privately, and investing in this and not expecting anyone else to foot the bill motivated me to work hard at fixing myself.

And my therapist helped me do that. She was patient, kind, and supportive. She saw me at my worst but enabled me to find the path to become my best.

I want to share my story with you because mental health affects each of us differently. My experience of depression and anxiety differs from how someone else experiences it. That doesn't make either of us better or worse off than the other; it's just different. But, left unchecked, mental health issues can severely detriment our lives.

According to MIND, a mental health charity in England, mental health issues affect one in four people yearly. That is a lot of people out there struggling with daily life because of something that can't be seen. And it stops us from living the life we want and deserve. It keeps us in a place of fear and hopelessness, so we never move forward. We can't create the life we want if we don't look at our mental health — and if it is not allowing us to move forward, we need to be able to do something about it.

Limiting beliefs are the number-one way I've seen mental health affect my clients and those around me. People accept these beliefs that they're not good enough, qualified enough, competent enough, or don't have the finances to take things forward in their lives. When my clients and I have looked deeper at these beliefs, they see that they're inaccurate. Working on these limiting beliefs has released them into being able to create lives they have only dreamed about.

Many people let their mental health issues define who they are. I used to do it too. I spoke about myself being depressed and anxious, taking on those qualities in all areas of my life. But this wasn't true. I wasn't depressed; I was *experiencing* depression. I wasn't anxious; I was *experiencing* anxiety. Even that slight change in narrative allowed me to move forward.

Depression and anxiety were not my personality. They were emotions and symptoms I experienced at different times in my life. I may well experience depression again. I still experience anxiety from time to time, but I have learned the signs and how to best manage them so that I can continue with my life.

It's worth noting that I've only spoken about depression and anxiety here because those are the mental health issues I personally have experienced. And these are *my* experiences. I'm not a mental health professional, and I'm not someone who has the experience or knowledge to opine about other mental health issues.

I have to thank that work colleague who initially raised the subject of depression with me. If they hadn't been courageous enough to mention it, my life might have turned out very differently.

FINAL THOUGHT

We must pay attention to our mental health and well-being to achieve our goals and dreams. Therapy helped me do this, but it may not be something everyone needs. Sometimes our feelings of being depressed or anxious are tied explicitly to specific situations instead of childhood trauma or chemical imbalances in our brains. Perhaps you only need support from someone who can show you the way out of the problem, allowing you to return to your pre-depressed or pre-anxious state.

If you experience mental health issues, I encourage you to seek help in a way that feels safe and productive, whether through counselling or therapy, a trauma-informed coach, NLP (Natural Language Processing) practitioner, or any other mental health professional.

Looking Ahead

If you have managed to work through Parts 1-3 and have completed the prompts, then you are a rock star! We tackle the final Part 4, *The Way*

Forward, with *7 Steps to Authentic Living* (Chapter 11), *7 Daily Practices for Lifetime Change* (Chapter 12), explore continued growth in Chapter 13, and then wrap things up with my closing thoughts in Chapter 14. Don't stop now, you're in the homeward stretch!

PART FOUR

The Way Forward

CHAPTER ELEVEN:

7 STEPS FOR AUTHENTIC LIVING (AKA BE TRUE TO YOU)

Authenticity is about being true to who you are, even when everyone around you wants you to be someone else.

— Michael Jordan

E VERY PERSON you've ever met has a version of you stored in their mind. But that version isn't usually the 'real' you because not many of us portray our most authentic selves to everyone at all times. The reverse also holds true: You've stored a version in your mind of everyone you've met, but the version of them you saw probably isn't entirely the real 'them' either.

All to say, we all wear masks depending on where we are or who we are with, and most of these masks or sides of us develop throughout the course of our lives.

As very young children, we're not armed with the filters or self-protection mechanisms we learn to use when we get older. And so we could say that we are our most authentic selves during this early period of life. We aren't worrying about if how we act or what we say is going to upset the person we are interacting with. We are operating from a liberated place, but as we grow up, we learn from those around us to adapt our behaviour to fit the situations we're in.

If you are a parent of school-age children, have you ever attended a parent-teacher evening at your child's school, where the teacher tells you that your child is attentive, helpful, and a pleasure to teach? You may wonder if the teacher is describing the same child! At home, your child is pushing boundaries, pushing your buttons, and pushing back on anything you ask them to do.

This is an excellent example of your child adapting to their situation (in this case, learning to respect authority in a peer setting), and this will continue for your child as they grow, when they go to university, get a job, join social groups, and start dating.

Speaking of dating, has anyone ever told you that you've 'changed' when you started dating someone new? It's natural to take on the personality traits of people we spend a lot of time with. But sometimes, in doing this, we lose or hide parts of ourselves — either to make the relationship succeed or to not face rejection from our new partner.

Consider fitting in with work colleagues. We don't necessarily take on traits of people we work with. Still, we may hide parts of ourselves that others might not find palatable to help create a pleasant working environment.

Hiding like this can be tiring because we are, in essence, playing a character. We are not our authentic selves, and it takes energy to keep playing a different part to different people. This is why you may feel drained after seeing certain people or being in specific situations.

I know I've felt this way before. I've hidden sides of me I felt wouldn't meet people's expectations and toned down my behaviour or beliefs to divert judgement from my peers. It comes down to wanting to be liked and validated, but when I did find the courage to share more sides of myself with friends, they were pleasantly surprised. And I've reacted the same way when friends and colleagues start to share more of themselves with me.

'Oh, I didn't know you liked crystals!'

'I never took you for being into rap music!'

Just as we learn to use such filters as we grow to keep from revealing our whole selves to others, we learn to stop caring so much about those filters as we age. As the saying goes, 'It's none of your business what others think of you.'

We stop caring about what others think and experience refreshing freedom in living from a place of genuine authenticity. Wouldn't it be great to realise this before we reach a certain age?

But what does it mean to live an authentic life, and how does it empower us? Being authentic doesn't mean telling everyone you meet everything about yourself. It also doesn't mean telling people precisely what you think of them in the spirit of tough love.

Instead, living authentically is about speaking your truth when necessary. It's about sticking up for what you believe in. It's about not trying to fit in with everyone else if that doesn't feel good for you. It means having integrity and living in alignment with the standards you set for yourself — and that's what we'll examine in this chapter.

THE BENEFITS OF LIVING AUTHENTICALLY

Ask yourself this: If there was zero chance of anyone judging you, disliking you, or cutting you out of their life, would you speak your mind and act in a way that was your truth? There is no right or wrong answer:

- Some of us would answer COMPLETELY and go about our day speaking our truth.

- Others might answer MAYBE because they're still holding onto the belief that they can control how others think about them.

- And some would answer NO because they're so wrapped up in being the version that everyone else sees that they don't know their truth to be able to speak it!

If you answered 'Completely' or even 'Maybe,' you might think that being authentic is just about being yourself, right? How hard can it really be to start acting 100% as yourself?

Well, there's a bit more to it than that. None of us stops being who we currently are overnight. It takes time to peel back the layers of expectations, societal conditioning, and pressures we've allowed others to pile on us.

To live in alignment with your true self, you'll have to do a fair bit of work to get there. You must be self-aware and willing to learn more about yourself. And you must learn to accept yourself regardless of how society or others perceive you. This is not easy work. You will discover parts of yourself that you had forgotten and new pieces you didn't realise existed. You will have to traverse the shadows of places you may have once ignored, and the journey won't be quick.

Ready to sign up yet?

Here's why living authentically is so important: When we live as our authentic selves, we let go of stagnant and negative energy that is not our own.

People pleasing or acting in the best interests of others instead of ourselves leave imprints in our own Soul and energy. It creates resistance, and life doesn't seem to flow as easily — because this energy isn't ours.

When we start living authentically, our energy is our own. It flows, and it attracts what we desire into our lives. We learn to trust ourselves so that we can connect with the Universe and others in more profound and trusting ways. Living authentically attracts other authentic people to you.

Everything you've read so far in this book leads back to living as your authentic self, from your Treasure Chest and manifestation to tapping into your Higher Self and establishing your daily practices. To create a life you love, you will need to be your authentic self. Anything else will feel forced or unfulfilling.

7 STEPS FOR AUTHENTIC LIVING

Now that you better understand the benefits of living authentically, I'm providing a roadmap of seven steps to get there. Each step includes a prompt for you to contemplate and answer.

1. Identify your beliefs about yourself.

Do you believe things about yourself that simply aren't true? What is the 'Story of You' you repeatedly tell yourself, or what is on those old tapes in your head that you play on repeat?

Examples:

'I'm not good enough.'

'I'm too lazy to reach my goal.'

'I'm not a good friend.'

What we believe about ourselves feeds into how we behave around others. We might make ourselves small to avoid bringing attention to certain aspects of our personalities or overcompensate to erase these traits.

Take some time to write down on a piece of paper all of your beliefs about yourself, both positive and negative. If you feel called to, once you have this written out, burn this piece of paper, thanking your beliefs for getting you so far, and then releasing your old beliefs with it.

2. Reflect on the belief systems held by your family.

Much of what we learn and how we show up in the world comes from our families' belief systems. After all, that's where we are first taught how to behave. And for those who grew up in a religious or particularly strict family, these beliefs can be amplified. They play into practically every aspect of who we are, even if we don't resonate with what we're being taught. We don't challenge these beliefs when we are young because our world is relatively small. But when we start school, university and work, we meet people from different walks of life, and interacting with them can make us question how we were raised. This is not uncommon; in fact, it's totally natural!

Spend time journalling about your family of origin's belief systems and how they've shaped you. Do you carry these beliefs with you today because they resonate, or have you shed some or all of these?

3. Have compassion for yourself.

We're not always good at offering ourselves kindness or grace, especially during difficult times. We'd never dream of treating others as poorly as we do ourselves, would we?

Part of stepping fully into our authentic selves requires a great deal of self-compassion. It's not easy to switch from that constant and critical internal monologue to a soothing voice of loving acceptance. As you work to get to the root of what it means for you to live as your most authentic self, you may revert to old behaviours because that's what feels comfortable. If you do, that's okay. Give yourself that grace. No matter how hard we try to change for the better, a lifetime's worth of conditioning can rear its ugly head! It will take some time to tame it.

How can you offer yourself compassion today? What are three kind things you can say to yourself right now? Write them down and keep them somewhere handy to refer to when needed.

4. Notice how you act (or react) in situations.

Who *hasn't* been in a conversation where, upon reflection, we would have done or said things differently? When in a stressful situation, our emotions can take over, and our conscious thinking can desert us. It's easy to act on emotion because most of us have been taught to react that way.

If you're serious about wanting to live authentically, you have no choice but to reflect on how you act in various situations. Learn what language you use to express yourself during difficult conversations. Is what you say kind, necessary, and true? Do you think about your words before speaking so that you can best convey what's on your heart in a gentle and non-judgemental way?

This approach also applies when we might initially choose not to speak or act but, on reflection, wish we had spoken up — especially if it is in defence of ourselves or something we believe in or are passionate about.

Think back on a recent conversation or situation when you wish you would have responded or acted differently. Write down your thoughts, including any different approaches you could have used. How would this different approach better match your genuine intention in that situation?

5. Explore your core values.

Our core values — the things that matter most to us and the behaviours we wish to live by — can be the most significant indicators of our authentic selves. They help us define our moral purpose in life. Living according to our core values allows us to experience profound personal fulfilment and make better life decisions.

Taking time to reflect on our values lets us decide if they are *our* values or those placed on us by others. Did you know you're allowed to change your values? Nothing is set in stone! Just because you believed something yesterday doesn't mean you have to live by that today. This isn't wishy-washy. Instead, you may have gained new knowledge or a new perspective that causes you to shift your actions and beliefs. Life is about growth. I'd be more worried if you didn't allow yourself to explore and readjust your values on your life's journey.

List the three most important things in your life right now. Try not to overthink it. If you're having difficulty identifying just three, write down up to ten important things and rate them in order of priority. For the three highest-ranked items, do you implement them in your daily life, or do you just give lip service to them? Alternatively, what values are you holding onto that you want to shed or replace?

6. Release old behavioural patterns and belief systems.

Our patterns of behaviour and belief systems grow and change over time. We first learn them from our family and then from the wider world as we attend school and mix with people from different backgrounds. As we carry on through life, we may pick up or discard certain behaviours and beliefs based on who we spend time with and what we do.

There is nothing wrong with this, but once we become aware of behaviours or beliefs we wish to change, we have two choices. We can either work to change these or continue in the hope that somehow our life and the outcomes will change.

You've likely heard that the definition of insanity is doing the same thing repeatedly, expecting a different result. This is to say, if you desire change, you need to change your actions. You can embark on this work alone, but I'd encourage you to find a coach or therapist for support. The help of an unbiased person can help you achieve more transformative results, bringing you closer to your authentic self.

Take time to reflect on the ingrained patterns and beliefs you wish to shed. How have these been serving you? How would your authentic self be better served by letting these go?

7. Give yourself time.

There is no prompt for this step. Simply remember that this deep Soul work takes time, and it's not something you can knock out in a weekend. The deeper you go, the more you'll find additional layers that can be difficult and painful to uncover. This fact alone prevents some from even starting this personal excavation work. But if you keep sharing yourself authentically, you'll be able to create a life you love.

FINAL THOUGHT: DON'T GIVE UP!

As you work on being true to yourself, you might be questioned about your changed behaviour or standards.

Why don't you want to go out partying anymore?

When did you become so spiritual?

When your 'real' self starts to emerge, you will find that some people won't accept it or are repelled by it. Instead, they will try to revert you to the version of you that they can relate to.

This is where I say, 'Don't give up!' You keep yourself small and your light dimmed by reverting to a former, less real version of you. Your Soul is not here for that to happen! Your Soul is here to be your most genuine self, even if that means losing a few people along the way.

Yes, it's scary! I've been there. As I embarked on this journey, I lost close friendships, and when we met again a few years later, we no longer had a connection. As my confidence in my true self grew, I mourned those friendships less and less. This is a result of the continued work that brings me closer to my authentic self — and this will be true for you too.

As you continue down the right path for your life, you'll meet other travellers on a similar journey, and some of these people may become friends. It's important to connect with them to offer each other support.

In closing, I'll let you in on two secrets:

1. We often do things in life so that others will like us.

2. It's okay for people not to like you.

These two secrets together create a paradox or situation that combines contradictory truths. We work hard to do things to get people to like and validate us. But then we end up not liking ourselves and all we do to gain this acceptance.

It's okay for others to not like you. It's <u>not</u> okay for *you* to not like you!

CHAPTER TWELVE:
7 DAILY PRACTICES FOR LIFETIME CHANGE

You'll never change your life until you change something you do daily. The secret to your success is found in your daily routine.

— John C. Maxwell

I'VE WRITTEN a great deal about how everything you desire is already here for you, that manifesting what you want takes action, that you need to be your authentic self to achieve what you want, and how you might encounter blocks when you start to change your life. All of this is food for your Soul, but how do you anchor into the person you need to be?

In Chapter 3, I mentioned that when I researched how successful people had created their lives in a way that worked for them, they listed the importance of a daily practice at the top of their lists. They did certain things each day to keep them on their intended path to live the life they wanted.

So, what exactly is a daily practice? Put simply, it can be one or multiple things you do daily to ground yourself and remind yourself of your purpose. You can incorporate it into your morning routine, turn it into an evening reflection, or use it to break up your day.

Whatever you choose, a daily practice is like a love letter to yourself. It's a declaration that you want to choose yourself and how you want to live your life. Your daily practice is the thing that nourishes your Soul so that you can be the best version of yourself. It allows you to fill up your cup first so that you can easily pour into others. Having had this practice for a while, I sometimes find that on days when I don't incorporate some practice, I feel less grounded, and life feels a little more difficult.

Imagine starting your day doing things that leave you inspired and with more energy. Imagine ending your day feeling fulfilled and peaceful. Incorporating practices into your daily life can help you to do this.

When I started my daily practice, I tried quite a few practices and tools, and I'll introduce you to seven practices I've come to value. I highlighted three of them as helpful manifestation tools in Chapter 5. As you build your own daily practice, you might find different tools or practices that align more with you. Whatever they are, I encourage you to always do what feels right because that is where you will see the results you desire.

MEDITATION

Meditation is a way of bringing to consciousness that which is unconscious. It is not about clearing your mind of all thoughts — a common misconception leading to many people giving up meditation before they've felt the benefits! Instead, it helps focus your thoughts and promotes relaxation and stress reduction, something many of us need in this busy world.

There are many ways to meditate. You don't need to sit cross-legged on the floor with incense burning around you! Mindfulness, movement, and walking meditation are just a few ways meditation can be practised. As with everything, pick something that feels good for you so you don't feel forced into what you are doing.

I practice meditation almost every day. I sit with my eyes closed and let my inner world talk to me. I don't play background music or light candles or incense to set any ambience, though this is something that others enjoy. It is purely me, my Soul, and my Higher Self. Sometimes my Inner Child comes along when she feels left out!

Meditation is an integral part of my day, but it didn't come easily to me. My therapist encouraged me to meditate daily when I was diagnosed with clinical depression. It wasn't natural at first because my mind never wanted to shut up (remember that misconception I was talking about!). But with practice, I eventually spent twenty to thirty minutes each evening meditating. Sometimes I'd meditate so deeply that I'd fall asleep and wake up the next morning.

Once my depression eased, I stopped meditating because I thought I was fixed. I only started to practice it again as part of my yoga teacher training — and slipping back into it was challenging! On teacher training days, we were required to sit in silence for forty-five minutes before starting our day. I would fidget, get pins and needles in my legs, and my back would ache.

I knew I had to go back to the beginning of my practice, so I started with a few minutes a day for a week and then slowly increased it. Before long, I was back to thirty minutes of daily meditation. I try to meditate for fifteen to thirty minutes each day, but even if I can only fit in ten minutes, the benefits keep me going: less stress, better sleep, and a deep sense of peace and joy every single day!

A note on guided meditations: I have practised and led others in guided meditations, but they're not part of my daily meditation practice. I usually reserve them for when I want to reach a deeper level of my unconscious mind or if I'm being led in a practice by another teacher, coach, or healer.

Resources:

Please see the Resources section for books on meditation. Other resources you may find useful:

- Insight Timer App (found on the Apple Store)

- www.headspace.com

- www.calm.com

CREATING AN ALTAR

Altars traditionally are used for worship, sacrifice, or prayer in many religions. However, altars can also be very personal areas in our homes for practising gratitude, giving blessings, or setting intentions for ourselves and our lives.

Why set up or create an altar? It can be used as a sacred space for you to declare the intentions you have in creating the life that you want. You can visit this space to remind yourself of what you are working towards or use it as a place to pray, manifest, and give thanks for what your Soul is already receiving.

I'd long believed that altars were meant for worshipping something or someone. And since I'm not in the game of worshipping in that sense, altars always put me off. I've since come to understand that altars can be used in a powerful way to honour myself, something I'm working on, or something I value.

I've been unconsciously creating an altar for several years, where, after I meditate, I light incense or a candle and say a short prayer. This helps ground me and reminds me that I'm not here by accident. Everything I do and everything that transpires comes through the Universe to me. But I recently realised that this is something my mum has always done, creating an altar of sorts on the mantelpiece at home with religious texts and pictures, and lighting incense every morning. Who knew that this was already part of my upbringing!

This past year, I created my first intentional altar. I participated in a visioning exercise at the beginning of the year, and the word *LOVE* came to me in meditation, along with a white rose. This exercise encouraged me to adopt these as my word and flower of the year and to create a simple altar to bring awareness to love in a physical form.

So I did. I placed rose quartz crystals (representing love) on my little altar and a rose-scented candle that I lit for at least five minutes each day to consider how I wanted to bring more love into my life. This wasn't necessarily about finding a romantic relationship but showing myself more love and compassion. I also committed to buying fresh white roses every month to place on my altar.

This altar has proven to be a beautiful addition to my spiritual practices. It has helped me focus on love (and play with what that means to me), and it has also connected me more deeply with my Soul and what it wants for me.

Resources:

My intentional altar came from a visioning exercise that I did in a workshop with oracle creator, writer and devotional creative Rebecca Campbell. You can find more information on her website below:

https://rebeccacampbell.me/how-to-make-an-altar/

Deepak Chopra also has a comprehensive guide on his website:

https://chopra.com/articles/sacred-space-how-to-make-an-altar-in-your-home

JOURNALLING

Have you ever had thoughts running through your mind that you wish you could pull out and make sense of? Or have you had so many ideas and plans that you don't know which one to work on first? If so, journalling may be the practice you need!

Spending even a few minutes each day writing whatever comes to your mind can clear the chaos in your head, whether that's in the morning so your day starts the way you want it to, or at the end of the day to let go of what has happened during the day so you can wind down for a good night's sleep.

I try to journal most days, as it's a great tool to help me work through anything I'm trying to process. There's something about writing down how I'm feeling, my options, or the pros and cons of a decision that helps me clear away the clutter in my mind.

Journalling is also an excellent way for me to access my Soul. I like to ask my Soul what it would like from the day and if there's something it wants me to explore. I let whatever comes to mind be transcribed on the page rather than trying to control what I write, tapping into my Soul and whatever guidance it has for me.

My tips for journalling:

1. Keep it simple.

2. Write as if no one is reading. This is about you and your feelings and thoughts when you write.

3. You don't only have to use words. Draw. Create a collage. Do whatever feels good for you.

4. Try to journal at the same time each day; it'll help you create a solid practice.

5. Buy a beautiful notebook or journal that will excite you to implement and develop this practice.

Resources:

My favourite journals are from Ottergami, available on Amazon.

GRATITUDE

Practising gratitude is a game-changer. Studies have shown that it creates greater happiness. Feeling grateful helps you to find joy in your experiences, and it can create more positive emotions. Gratitude also can bring about a sense of peace from appreciating your current life. It is also a key practice when it comes to manifestation.

I write down three or more things I'm grateful for as part of my daily journalling practice. They're not always big things; sometimes, I'm thankful the sun is shining, or it didn't rain on my walk to the gym. At first, it may seem impossible to find even a few things you're grateful for each day, but I promise the more you practise finding gratitude and joy every day, the more your eyes will open to all you have, and a heart of thankfulness will bloom within you.

I went through most of my life with a closed heart. I was approachable and friendly but rarely allowed myself to be vulnerable. I didn't want to risk the pain that comes from getting hurt. When I started practising gratitude, I felt my heart open and naturally allowed people to see me in my realness. This helped my confidence grow to where I could speak up for myself more. That is gratitude's domino effect, and you can experience it too.

Resources:

If you don't currently have a gratitude practice, I suggest visiting **https://www.mindful.org/an-introduction-to-mindful-gratitude/**

I haven't found any specific books on gratitude that I would recommend, but many of the self-help books I've read have all mentioned gratitude in one way or another. There are also many gratitude journals that you can purchase online that will take you through the steps of practising gratitude.

MOVING YOUR BODY

We all know that moving our bodies is essential, but it can feel like a chore — especially when we see limited activities presented as options for keeping our bodies in shape. You don't have to go to the gym or train for a marathon. You just need to find some movement you enjoy to keep doing it!

I've naturally enjoyed and incorporated movement into my daily life, whether walking, running, or practising yoga. That changed for me with the pandemic. Once I transitioned to working from home, I realised that walking from meeting to meeting in the office was replaced with a lot of sitting — and my smartwatch took notice of the reduced daily steps! So, I attempted to go for daily walks and keep up with my yoga practice to keep my body moving. But my work became more demanding, and extra meetings appeared on my calendar, cutting into my free time. After several weeks of this, I noticed the difference in my physical and mental health.

Now, I make it a priority to get in some daily movement, if for no other reason than to move the energy in my body around. If my energy feels stagnant, I can quickly get unmotivated or lazy. It's important to take a break to get moving; even a quick dance to your favourite song can shake things up and provide a second wind to get through the day!

Don't get disheartened if it takes a while to establish movement in your day, especially if it's something new for you or you're out of practice and are rediscovering a lost passion. Build up slowly or ask a friend or relative to join you so that you also get quality time with them. Who knows, they may have been wanting to do this all along!

Resources:

Many online classes are available, from yoga and Pilates to HIIT workouts and dance classes. There really does seem to be something for everyone. If you want something more local and in-person, search for clubs or classes that interest you, like walking or running clubs.

NOURISHMENT

Just as moving our body and taking care of our mind are essential, one thing connects them both — nourishment. The food we put inside our bodies is just as important as all the external factors in our daily practice.

Not only does food impact our physical well-being and ensure our body is functioning correctly, but it also affects our mood, energy levels, and mental health.

It's taken me a while to understand and appreciate that what I put inside my body affected every part of my life. I've mentioned my sugar addiction and my issues with alcohol throughout this book. Even when I was eating a healthy, balanced diet, these two things caused me to feel lethargic and unmotivated. Not a good combination when trying to create the life I wanted to live.

I rarely drink now and am still working on reducing my sugar intake (it's much better than before) because I know how good I feel when I don't have those things in my diet. Eating more natural versus processed food has also made a difference in my moods and energy levels. This all means that I can do the things I want to in life and not worry about that lethargic or demotivated feeling anymore.

If you struggle with your eating habits and want to ensure you nourish yourself in a way that lets you lead an active and fulfilled life, I recommend seeing a health coach or nutritionist. Books are plenty on this subject, but each of us is different and requires someone who can tailor eating plans and nutrition to our needs.

Resources:
www.integrativenutrition.com

ORACLE CARDS

Before I talk about how I use Oracle Cards, I want to briefly explain the difference between Oracle Cards and Tarot Cards. A Tarot Deck has a traditional structure and common meanings. So if you had a specific Tarot Deck, it would have the same cards and meanings as another Tarot Deck. Oracle Card Decks, however, can have any theme, purpose, and number of cards. They have a broader meaning than Tarot Cards, which are more detailed and focused.

I have several sets of Oracle Cards. Not only are they beautiful to look at, but they're fun and a pleasure to use. I pull a single card each morning to provide guidance or a simple message for my day. I also utilise them in a deeper card ritual on the monthly new and full moons. I know they're not everyone's thing, but they bring a bit of playfulness into my life. I've rarely pulled a card that didn't resonate with my feelings that day!

Don't worry if you're a beginner wondering how to use Oracle Cards. All Oracle Card Decks will come with a book explaining the meaning behind each card. The book will guide you in infusing the deck with your energy so that the cards you pull will be attuned to you. You will also get guidance on how to do different types of reading for yourself.

Resources:

Some of my favourite Oracle Card Decks:

A Yogic Path by Sahara Rose Ketabi

Work Your Light Oracle Cards by Rebecca Campbell

The Starseed Oracle by Rebecca Campbell

FINAL THOUGHT

My daily practice is a combination of everything I've shared here. In some way or another, these practices feature in my life every day. When I travel or am away from home, I may not get to do all of them, and I sometimes adjust how I do them, but they are there, filling up my cup.

Be gentle with yourself when creating a daily practice. Perhaps try one thing at a time and slowly bring in other elements. Always remember, though, to do what feels good for YOU. A daily practice is not a chore or something used to punish yourself. Instead, it serves as a gentle reminder that you choose yourself, that your connection with yourself matters so that you can empower your Soul to live the life you're here to live.

Having read through this chapter, think about and write down your reflections on a daily practice:

1. Do you currently have a daily practice? If so, what do you incorporate into your day? Is it a morning or evening practice?

2. What practices would you like to explore and add to your daily practice?

3. If you don't have a daily practice, what one thing would you like to try to get yourself started?

CHAPTER THIRTEEN:
THERE IS ALWAYS ROOM FOR GROWTH

The only person you are destined to become is the person you decide to be.

— Ralph Waldo Emerson

I'VE SEEN PEOPLE on this personal development journey who, once they've landed on a version of their dream life, simply stop. They feel successful, satisfied and content. Then there are others who keep going even after they've reached their initial goals. They build more and create more. They don't stop.

Beautiful Soul, life is about living — not merely existing — which is likely why you chose to read this book. When people perceive they have achieved it all, they're just existing.

The people who keep going, keep living. They don't continue out of greed or obligation. Instead, their curiosity is piqued; they enjoy this new taste of life. Why would they want to stop that feeling? Once they can see the world in all its vivid technicolour, why would they revert to black and white?

When I look back at my experience of depression, I realise I did everything I could just to exist. Every day was a struggle. I didn't have hope or dreams because no one had taught me how to dream. By default, I had been taught to exist in the same box as everyone else, and my Soul knew that wasn't why I was here in this lifetime. It's not why your Soul is here, either.

That feeling of *existing* scares me, and I've experienced it a few times since those crippling depressive episodes. But this very feeling pushes me out of my comfort zone to try something new. It reminds me there is more for me — but I'm the only one who can reach out and grab it.

There's always room for us to grow and learn new things about ourselves and the world around us. We don't have to stop at a certain point. You are doing yourself and your Soul a disservice when you decide to stop because you *think* you are now happy. Just as a garden needs constant tending and attention, so does your Soul and its dreams. You may have reached one point, but maybe that was just the first point. Your Soul wanted to see how you handled things before it pushed you towards more.

Enjoy what you have and acknowledge all you've achieved, but please don't stop reaching for new experiences and dreams. This growth, this continued seeking, is what you are here for.

Don't forget: Your Soul is your guide. It's natural, even with new routines (possibly some borrowed from the previous chapter), to settle back into being a creature of habit. All you've really done is create a new comfort zone. Yes, it's further out than the last one, but you'll get cosy there pretty quickly. And if you're tuned into your Soul, you'll hear when it starts rumbling that it's time to try something new. Listen to it — because its voice will only grow louder to where you can no longer ignore it.

If you accept your Soul's charge to keep moving forward, it's important to remember three helpful travel tips — really, a piece of advice, a word of caution, and an encouragement — for your journey:

1. Take time to enjoy the journey.

2. The journey won't always be easy.

3. You *will* meet people like you on your journey.

MY ADVICE: TAKE TIME TO ENJOY THE JOURNEY

It can be easy to get carried away and want instant transformation when we start to make changes in our life. It's natural to want to see benefits in all areas of our life when we make gains in one area, but this change won't happen overnight. Creating a life you love is often a slow process.

It's tempting to want to see the final result before we've done the work to get there, but the *journey* of creating your life is where the good stuff lives! The ups and downs, the challenges, the discovery of new passions and places, and meeting new people — it's all part of the fun! Surely you don't want to miss out on all that to skip ahead to the end result?

In a *Diary of a CEO* podcast episode, host Steven Bartlett shared how he felt when his company went public on the stock exchange. It turns out he wasn't as excited or celebratory as he thought he'd be, even though he'd spent years building up his business to achieve this major milestone. He found greater satisfaction in his work to get there than in the end result.

That's how it is when we talk of creating our dream life. Ralph Waldo Emerson put it best when he said, 'It's not about the destination. It's about the journey.' There is always scope for change, and just because you've reached a certain point in your life you've been working for doesn't mean that you'll want to sit back and not create anything more for your life. That's what enjoying the journey is all about. In fact, you'll enjoy this journey so much that it will spur you to create even more joy and happiness in your life.

A CAUTION: IT WON'T ALWAYS BE EASY

You'll experience difficult times on your journey — full-on 'What the heck am I doing?' types of difficult times. It's happened to me a few times now. It slowly creeps up on me until I'm in full-fledged panic mode, and I start to second-guess myself:

Is what I'm doing worth it?

Is this really the right path for me to be taking?

Wouldn't it just be easier to turn around and keep doing what I'm doing instead of trying to change things to improve my life?

Those are the moments where I have slipped back into old ways and behaviours that didn't serve me then and certainly weren't serving me now. It's like that saying, 'Two steps forward, one step back.' I often felt like that before I got to where I am now.

And guess what? It is perfectly okay to feel like this. Change is never easy, especially when you're so invested. It's not a straight path from A to B. Expect a few detours where you find yourself in places you never imagined. The road may feel rocky, but it's worth it because it takes you where you want to go.

Keep your goals for your Big Life front and centre. Do you want to live mortgage-free? Do you wish to work for yourself? Maybe you want to be able to work from anywhere in the world. Each of these takes work and, often, sacrifice.

Remember, whatever is meant for your Soul is already done, and it's up to you to work towards it. And sometimes, that work feels difficult because you can't see the solution or a way around the challenge you're facing.

Those are the times you'll want to run away from what your Soul wants — but you have to stay. You must remain on the path because how could you live with yourself knowing you gave up on what you really wanted?

Another word of caution: Beware the roadblocks of others' opinions. People in your old life may want you to stay where you are and remain the person they know and love. But that isn't what your Soul is craving; it wants something different. Who truly matters? Your Soul, or the Souls of others?

By turning away from the life you're trying to create, you're choosing to help create another Soul's life. And your Soul did not sign up for that. Remember this every time you feel like you're straying away from what you're trying to create. (Feel free to read that again and let it sink in.)

I've cried many times when I found stepping forward more painful than continuing on as I was. A journey of self-discovery is ultimately a journey of healing, and the emotions that can surface can feel unexpected and confusing. Surely you should feel nothing but light and bright all the time, right? It doesn't work like that. When you realise how badly you want to change your life and create something you love waking up to each day — when you allow yourself to be spurred on by this difficult feeling — this helps you keep moving toward your goal, no matter who or what you may have to leave behind.

BE ENCOURAGED: YOU *WILL* FIND PEOPLE LIKE YOU

As I've already mentioned, it can be difficult to release yourself from the attachments to some people in your life to create the life you want. Here's the good news: When you step with courage into the next level of your life, you will meet fellow travellers doing the same. Perhaps they are walking right alongside you, or maybe they're slightly ahead and have managed to get to the next stop along the bus route.

Why is this important? When you're surrounded by people rooted firmly in their comfort zone, that is all you'll see. You won't see the people who have stepped out of their comfort zone or hear how they dealt with the same challenges you're facing. You won't get to listen to the struggles they went through to get what they want. You won't learn how to get to where you're going more easily by learning from their example.

When I started my coaching business, I invested in programmes that allowed me to see how other people had successfully set themselves up as coaches. I tried emulating their techniques, but my coaching business wasn't taking off as much as I expected.

I was missing something, and as I saw it, I had two choices. I could plug away at how I'd been taught, or I could find a successful coach teaching others how to do the same. Thankfully, I didn't have to look far. I followed Preston Smiles, a seven-figure life coach on Instagram, though I didn't know he was a coach at the time. Around the time I discovered what he did, I was able to jump in on one of his webinars about mistakes new coaches make. I signed up and sat through a passionate dialogue about everything that keeps coaches struggling. That was what I was trying to avoid!

That was a good first step, leading me to a ten-week programme led by Preston Smiles and Zion Kim that taught me how to structure and build my coaching business, be of the best service to others, and put me in contact with other coaches who were that step ahead of me. That programme turned out to be one of the best decisions of my life. It led me to a community I could learn from and a community that I could also help. It connected me to others working towards the same goals I was.

Learning from your own mistakes is one thing, but when you have coaches teaching you by sharing their mistakes, that is something else. When I worked in the finance industry, not everyone was out to help as much as I thought they were. Some would help to a certain point but then stop when it meant I might overtake their progress. Others would help me with an agenda of ultimately helping themselves.

So, as you surround yourself with people who have been there, make sure they're genuine and really want to help you avoid the pitfalls they found on their journey. Look for people who have a strong connection with themselves and can offer support and friendship. Find people who want to see you win. I can't begin to describe how important this was for me. It allowed me to gain the confidence to explore my life and what I wanted. It allowed me to make mistakes and see how I could change other situations in my life.

Also, thanks to social media, your community doesn't need to live a few roads away from you anymore. Your community is out there, online, ready for you to connect and share yourself and your journey with them. A lot of my community is in the virtual world, and I am beyond grateful for the people I have met. I wouldn't be where I am now without their support and influence. They are the types of people I spoke about before. Go out there, even into the virtual space, and find your community. It is a crucial (and rewarding) piece of the puzzle to create the life you want to live.

Find these people because they will be the ones who get you out of your comfort zones. They will be the ones who will show you that there is another way and assure you that you're on the right path to creating the life you deserve.

Find them, I dare you!

FINAL THOUGHT

A self-development journey is not always the easiest task for us to undertake. We can become so focused on the outcomes or goals that we forget to enjoy the present moment and what we are experiencing. We don't always see what we are learning about ourselves and others as we go on our journey because we look too far ahead to what we want to achieve.

Our memories and the thoughts we share with others as we reminisce over that cup of coffee or glass of wine can only be made if we let ourselves really experience what we are going through. We can tap back into the joy and celebrate ourselves over and over again in this way. Don't let your focus on the outcome blur the journey you are on. Enjoy the present for the gift it is!

Think back to a time when you were presented with a challenge or goal:

1. What did you experience whilst dealing with that challenge or pursuing that goal?

2. What did you learn from your experience?

3. How did that experience improve you and
    your skills and talents?

CHAPTER FOURTEEN:
CLOSING THOUGHTS

The future belongs to those who believe in the beauty of their dreams.

— Eleanor Roosevelt

I NO LONGER dread the sound of my alarm clock. Instead of going to a job I don't enjoy, I wake up to spend the day in whatever way my Soul desires.

Movement is first up, and I enjoy the walk to the gym for my morning workout. This time of day is so peaceful, something I never truly appreciated when rushing to catch the bus or train to work. The world is just starting to stir from its slumber. Whilst working out, I listen to an audiobook or podcast, currently *That Little Voice In Your Head* by Mo Gawdat. As I walk back home, the daily bustle has begun. People are on their way to work or school, but I am on my way home.

Once I've showered and dressed, I make space for my daily meditation and altar practice to help ground my energy for the rest of the day. I enjoy a leisurely breakfast and review client requests and interactions over a cup of tea before journalling and pulling an Oracle Card to set my intention for the day. Although I spend time planning out tasks and meetings each week, I still ask my Soul what it wants.

I recall the first story about myself that I shared with you in this book:

'I'd wake up each morning and go to my 9-to-5 job, join in office banter, talk about TV shows and what was for dinner, and gossip about other people. As soon as I clocked off, I'd be back on a train home to an evening of watching TV, numbing my emotions with food, and ignoring how depressed and sad I felt. Of course, social events,

family gatherings, work commitments, and holidays served as a distraction. But on the whole, this is how my life had panned out.'

What a far cry my life is from that time — and I'm not finished. My life feels more purposeful, and I do work that brings me flexibility and enjoyment. I have time for the people I love, plus time for travel. Now that I know what I'm capable of manifesting, I want more — more travel, more new friendships, more inner exploration and growth. It's all there for the taking, isn't it?

I may reach a point and determine that I'm content, or I may want to change things up once again. The thing is, I get to decide and embark on that journey again and again. I choose to let my Soul direct me closer to the desires and gifts in my Treasure Chest.

I'm more than aware that I'll continue to face challenges along the way, but life is about adaptation and growth. I believe that if we take care to embody the fullest version of ourselves, then we remain the driving force in our lives instead of letting ourselves be tossed to and fro by life's prevailing winds.

I wish all of this and so much more for you, beautiful Soul! Thank you for choosing to include me in your journey toward creating the life you love. I sincerely hope that this book has been helpful in even the slightest way. I would love to hear more about your own journey, including the obstacles you've come up against and the exciting breakthroughs you've experienced. Please feel free to email me at TheEmpoweredSoulBook@gmail.com or send me a message at my website's contact form (www.harmeschkaur.com).

Just as I've ended each chapter with a final thought, I wish to leave you with a few closing thoughts to conclude our work together in this book:

1. **This is only the beginning.** As we come to the close of this book, and after working through the 100+ prompts I've provided, I'm sure you realise that redesigning your life is truly a lifelong endeavour. You're working toward a long-term vision, not a short-term fix, so just as I suggested at the beginning of this book, I encourage you to take your time.

2. **Make it a joyful journey!** Life is for living, so do take time to revel in the excitement of it all. If you let it, you're literally in for the adventure of a lifetime!

3. **The ripple effect is real, rewarding — and your responsibility.** Please know: As you change things in your life, they'll have

a ripple effect on the people around you, and that ripple can be positive! Once people see you feeling happier, having more fun, and feeling that spark for life again, they'll want to know *your* secret. They will want to see *how* you did it. They will want to learn where they can find this magic you've discovered.

And now you'll know just what to tell them.

Much love,

Harmesch

RESOURCES

I AM SHARING just a few of the books and resources that I have used and which have either made a significant impact on me and how I choose to live my life, or helped me on my journey. Hopefully, you might also find them helpful.

BOOKS

Bell, Andy. The DIY Investor: How to Take Control of Your Investments and Plan for a Financially Secure Future. Harlow, UK: Pearson Education Limited, 2013

Chopra, Deepak. The Seven Spiritual Laws Of Success: A Practical Guide To The FulFilment Of Your Dreams. London, UK: Bantam Press, 1996

Clear, James. Atomic Habits: An Easy & Proven Way to Build Good Habits & Break Bad Ones. London, UK: Penguin Random House UK, 2018

Coelho, Paulo. The Alchemist. London, UK: HarperCollins, 1993

Estes, Clarissa Pinkola. Women Who Run With The Wolves: Contacting The Power Of the Wild Woman. London, UK: Rider, 1992

Falconer, Erin. How to Get Sh*t Done: Why Women Need To Stop Doing Everything So They Can Achieve Anything. New York, N.Y.: Gallery Books, 2018

Gilbert, Elizabeth. Big Magic: Creative Living Beyond Fear. London, UK: Bloomsbury, 2015

Hay, Louise. You Can Heal Your Life. London, UK: Hay House Ltd., 1984

His Holiness the Dalai Lama. Stages of Meditation. The Buddhist Classic on Training the Mind. Boulder, Colorado: Shambhala Publications, Inc. 2002

Keller, Gary: The One Thing: The Surprisingly Simple Truth Behind Extraordinary Results. London, UK: John Murray (Publishers), 2013

Knight, Sarah. You Do You: How to Be Who You Are and Use What You've Got to Get What You Want. London, UK: Quercus Editions Ltd, 2017

Singer, Michael A. The Untethered Soul: The Journey Beyond Yourself. Oakland, CA: New Harbinger Publications, 2007

Twist, Lynne. The Soul of Money: Transforming Your Relationship with Money and Life. New York, NY: W. W. Norton, 2003, 2017

COACHES & COACHING INSTITUTIONS

Preston Smiles: www.prestonsmiles.com and Instagram: @prestonsmiles

Participation in Preston's programmes has been one of my best decisions, both personally and professionally. My involvement in his transformational coaching programme Stretch 22 led me to write this book.

Dharma Coaching Institute: www.dharmacoachinginstitute.com

ICF accredited training to become a Soul Purpose Life Coach.

International Coaching Federation: www.coachingfederation.org

The leading global organisation for coaches and coaching.

ORGANISATIONS & OTHERS

CITIZENS ADVICE:

www.citizensadvice.org.uk

National and local charity helping people with knowledge and confidence to find their way forward with life.

MIND:

www.mind.org.uk

UK Mental Health charity

SAMARITANS:

www.samaritans.org

Charity dedicated to reducing feelings of isolation and disconnection which can lead to suicide.

ACKNOWLEDGEMENTS

With thanks to:

My parents, for supporting my Soul to live the way it intended in this lifetime.

My sisters and brothers, for being exactly who you are, so I could be exactly who I am.

Kristi Runge for helping me to bring this book to life. For your patience, your guidance and your ideas. You've made the editing journey easy and a pleasure to be on.

Preston Smiles, Miriam Brewer, Michelle Mor and Renata DeMelo for creating and holding the sacred space in Stretch 22 that allowed this book to begin its journey.

Brooke Dinse McCarrison, Jess Jhoti, Chomps Kaeowsri, Laniece Herron, and Jen O'Farrell. I appreciate all of the time you gave to read through this book and provide your many insights. Your input, feedback and support has, and is, beyond words.

Anna Andrzejewski, Anne Lea Esch, and Laniece Herron, my Stretch 22 sisters, for all of your unspoken support.

All of my coaches, mentors and fellow coaches who have supported me, helped me to learn and to grow, and continue to do so as my Soul experiences the life it is here to enjoy.

Much love,

Harmesch

ABOUT THE AUTHOR

GROWING UP in a Sikh household in 1970s and '80s England, Harmesch Kaur was expected to fulfil her family's life purpose for her: Enter an arranged marriage, settle down, and have children. After all, that's what every woman in her family and community had done.

After multiple unsuccessful introductions to prospective marriage partners, Harmesch decided to forego continued humiliation and forge her own path. But with no preparation for life beyond marriage, what were her options?

Harmesch spent twenty years searching for answers, juggling a clinical depression diagnosis with her struggle to fit in with her Sikh culture and find her place in the modern Western world. Her journey initially led her on a working holiday in New Zealand and to work abroad in Switzerland, giving her a glimpse of spiritual purpose that she was drawn to but abandoned to pursue a corporate career in finance.

After building a fifteen-year career as a business analyst, Harmesch declared she wanted to exit the corporate world by age fifty. Even with her achievements, the 9-to-5 life ultimately proved unfulfilling. She knew there must be more to life. She was at a pivotal crossroads, and in 2019, the Universe directed her towards a turning point.

Harmesch took a remote job working for the Australian Stock Exchange from her home base in London. Working evening hours with her days free gave her a new perspective on how different life can be outside the 9-to-5 daily grind.

Harmesch had made the bold leap as a young adult to forge her own path outside of her Sikh culture, but she realised that, in a way, she had traded Sikh life and its traditions for a corporate life full of similar unreachable expectations. She had tackled some personal demons and made significant strides in life along the way, but with her fiftieth birthday fast approaching, she realised she was being called to go deeper and finally discover her purpose and create the life she was meant to live.

Just as the COVID-19 pandemic hit the world stage, Harmesch was able to start her transition out of the corporate world and pursue a new career as a life coach. A graduate of The Dharma Coaching Institute, Preston Smiles' Stretch 22 programme, and trained in Human Design, she now manages a thriving coaching and Human

Design business, with more books and courses in the pipeline.

Harmesch has broken free from the personal and professional constraints of an overwhelmingly prescriptive family culture and the high-stress, competitive world of finance. Now, she helps others clear their own life hurdles to find their purpose and experience the lives their Souls are here to live.

When she's not coaching clients or writing, Harmesch enjoys nature walks, photography, reading, and travelling the world, though she'll be the first to tell you that she's finally living a life she no longer needs a holiday from.

Follow Harmesch Kaur on social:

FB: https://www.facebook.com/HarmeschKaurCoach

IG: @harmesch.kaur

Website: www.harmeschkaur.com

Email: TheEmpoweredSoulBook@gmail.com

Printed in Great Britain
by Amazon

19938437R00215